The Inner World of Unaware Phenomena

The Inner World of Unaware Phenomena

Pathways to Brain, Behavior, and Implicit Memory

Bruce J. Diamond, Amy E. Learmonth, and Katherine Makarec

LEXINGTON BOOKS
Lanham • Boulder • New York • London

Published by Lexington Books
An imprint of The Rowman & Littlefield Publishing Group, Inc.
4501 Forbes Boulevard, Suite 200, Lanham, Maryland 20706
www.rowman.com

86-90 Paul Street, London EC2A 4NE

British Library Cataloguing in Publication Information Available

Library of Congress Cataloging-in-Publication Data

Names: Diamond, Bruce J., author. | Learmonth, Amy E., author. | Makarec, Katherine, author.
Title: The inner world of unaware phenomena: pathways to brain, behavior, and implicit memory / Bruce J. Diamond, Amy E. Learmonth, and Katherine Makarec.
Description: Lanham: Lexington Books, [2023] | Includes bibliographical references and index.
Identifiers: LCCN 2022031475 (print) | LCCN 2022031476 (ebook)
| ISBN 9781498555470 (cloth) | ISBN 9781498555494 (paper) | ISBN 9781498555487 (ebook)
Subjects: LCSH: Subliminal perception. | Preferences (Philosophy)
| Thought and thinking.
Classification: LCC BF323.S8 D53 2023 (print) | LCC BF323.S8
(ebook) | DDC 153.7/36—dc23/eng/20220720
LC record available at https://lccn.loc.gov/2022031475
LC ebook record available at https://lccn.loc.gov/2022031476

Contents

Acknowledgments

We would like to acknowledge the editorial support of Amanosi Agbugui, Jordyn Yeshion, Rebecca R. Pavlick, Melissa Gizzi and Jaclyn Ellis.

Introduction

Memories Lost and Memories Found

This text is about an exploration into the deepest recesses of our mind. That, perhaps, sounds a bit cliché. But it is certainly a journey, as we seek memories lost and memories found and how our lives are influenced by experiences, memories, and learning, about which we may be totally unaware, but, nevertheless, alter the quality, substance and trajectory of our lives.

Freud's view of the unconscious as a determinant of motivation and behavior was, in fact, revolutionary and the model that views the unconscious as a result of repression and trauma is expanding to include implicit, procedural, pre-symbolic and sub-symbolic forms of memory (Erskine, 2008). While there is a nexus between models, this text will be concerned with the idea of "cognitive unawareness" or the "non-conscious" world rather than the traditional psychoanalytic idea of the unconscious.

Freud viewed the unconscious as a vault in the mind where emotional and trauma-related experiences are stored and often forgotten. We suggest that the vault can be opened and that experiences are not necessarily "forgotten" or locked away in a sealed and impenetrable vault, but are, in fact, expressed in various ways and contexts at different times in our lives. Our journey encompasses the inner world of non-conscious phenomena, including information, learning, associations, experiences and memories that permeate our everyday lives, loves, likes and dislikes. Memories that, in many instances, are only expressed via implicit modalities.

It is a journey of self-discovery and the quest to better see and understand ourselves. It is also about the realization that so much of our lives is influenced by an inner world that is often cast in the shadows, yet has the potential to illuminate who we have been, who we are, and who we will be. This inner world lives within all of us, from infancy through old age, from the first to

1

the very last breath and it is a world that has the potential to bring us closer to ourselves.

BEHAVIORAL AND PHYSIOLOGICAL CORRELATES OF UNAWARE MEMORY

The defining characteristics of these implicit memories and their association to non-conscious processes was alluded to by the clinician Sergei Korsakoff in 1889 when he described a patient whom he had given an electrical shock. The patient had no explicit memory of the learning episode involving the shock. Interestingly, when the patient was shown a case that contained the shock apparatus, he reportedly said that Korsakoff had come to electrify him (Schacter, 1987).

The patient was not explicitly asked about the case but made his remark spontaneously. The question is how this patient knew that the case was associated with an electrical shock when he had no explicit memory of ever having been shocked. The extant literature suggests that this example is by no means an anomaly, as there is additional evidence supporting the fundamental idea that knowledge of the electrical shock can be preserved, and may be expressed in ways and in contexts that allow its expression despite the fact that the event could not be consciously recalled.

For example, research has demonstrated implicit perceptual knowledge in patients with brain damage. In visual agnosia, which is a disorder in which patients have difficulty perceiving and recognizing a wide variety of visual objects, there is a report in which a patient who was severely impaired in making judgments about the width of three-dimensional objects made entirely normal motor adjustments of her hand position as she reached toward a target object and made appropriate positional accommodations. In other words, the positioning of her finger-thumb grip varied directly as a function of the object's width despite the fact that she exhibited an impairment of conscious perception of the object (Goodale et al., 1991).

The answer may lie in the fact that this example and many similar ones demonstrate how the inner world of unaware phenomena can emerge in ways that influence behavior, but do so in ways that appear to be largely unknown to the individual. In terms of how this may occur, it is plausible that memories were, perhaps, weakly represented and while salient enough to influence behavior they were not sufficiently strong to be reflected in conscious and aware memory (Diamond, Mayes & Meudell, 1996; Schacter & Graf, 1989).

We will explore cases in the literature involving patients with amnesia and, in some instances, prosopagnosia, demonstrating the effects of unconscious processes and how these processes can impact our knowledge, beliefs, attitudes, and response to faces, places and memories in everyday life. More than anything, perhaps, we seek to illuminate that unaware world within all of us.

Chapter 1

Cognitive and Behavioral Indices of Unaware Phenomena across the Developmental Spectrum

EXPLICIT AND IMPLICIT MEMORY: DIGGING DEEPER INTO THE ABYSS

Memory influences behavior by the process of accessing prior experience of the world. Each new experience has the potential to influence behavior, and experiences that are similar to the current context are more likely to influence behavior. People may be conscious of the way memory is influencing their behavior, when, for example, they identify objects or people or talk about a past experience.

At other times, memory effects can influence behavior without the conscious awareness of the individual. So, for example, driving a car for the first time in several years, and making decisions about presented material faster and more accurately when the material was previously presented are behaviors that are influenced by memory without necessarily being aware of those memories or prior exposure.

Memory is divided into two broad types: explicit memory is recalled and available for conscious consideration, and implicit memory influences behavior but is not available to conscious awareness. Implicit memories, although not available to conscious examination, can have a powerful effect on behavior in a large number of situations. Much in our everyday lives is influenced by memories that do not reach the level of conscious awareness. Walking along a familiar path, we may avoid stepping on the uneven part of the sidewalk without even being consciously aware that the unevenness is there. Reaching for a coffee cup while writing does not take conscious planning, the only conscious part is the desire for a sip of coffee. These are all examples of implicit memory. Although I am sure many of you could not describe precisely where your coffee cup is on your desk, you can nevertheless reach for it unerringly.

Because of this lack of conscious awareness, much of the research into implicit memory uses tasks that are designed to show knowledge, memory or prior exposure to information through indirect means. For example, asking participants to complete a word-stem task in which the words they studied previously are used to complete the stem. Even if those same words are not consciously recalled, they are more likely to complete the word stems with words from the previously studied list (Hamann & Squire, 1997).

In other words, this shows implicit memory for the words, as participants are simply asked to fill in the word stem, rather than asked to explicitly recall the words. Blurry images that participants have seen before are identified more accurately and quickly than novel pictures, even if the participants have no conscious memory of the pictures (Drummey & Newcombe, 1995; Graf, Shimamura, & Squire, 1985). These kinds of tasks show that implicit memory has behavioral implications and that they provide a lens through which we can see into the inner world of unaware phenomena.

The differentiation between explicit and implicit memory is important from a theoretical perspective supporting the idea that these two kinds of memory are not just different levels of the same memory processes, but instead appear to represent separate memory systems each with their own features and neural circuits. Of clinical and functional importance is the fact that people with anterograde amnesia, a condition that interferes with the formation of new memories, can nevertheless show implicit memory.

In other words, patients with amnesia who did poorly on the explicit memory portion of the task (as would be predicted by their diagnosis) scored similarly to controls in word-stem completion, indicating some preservation of implicit memory (Warrington & Weiskrantz, 1982; Hamann & Squire, 1997; Graf et al., 1985). Likely, the most famous amnesia patient, HM, showed implicit memory in a number of different forms after a surgical procedure made most explicit forms of memory unavailable (Parkin, 1996).

From a methodological perspective there are experimental manipulations that generate different effects for implicit and explicit tasks. For example, if a word list is presented visually or aurally, the impact on explicit memory is negligible, but implicit memory performance appears to be better for visually presented word lists (Carlesimo, 1994; Carlesimo, Marfia, Loasses & Caltagirone, 1996). Interestingly, divided attention or interference with depth of processing of the study list interferes with explicit recall but has little to no impact on implicit memory (Schendan, 2019).

Implicit Processes in Infants and Children

Although word lists are not used with infants, there is evidence that infants have implicit memory. Infant memory for an event that has faded from explicit memory, operationalized by the infant no longer showing a learned behavior, can be reinstated by exposure to a small subset of the original event, much like the word stem completion in adults (Rovee-Collier, Hayne & Colombo, 2001; Learmonth, Cuevas & Rovee-Collier, 2015). The argument that implicit memory is available from early infancy with many of the features of the mature system implies that most of the developmental changes in memory occur within the explicit system (Rovee-Collier et al., 2001).

Infants and Procedural Memory

Infants show procedural memory from as early as they can be tested. The reflexes of early infancy become the skills completed with procedural memory as infants become more and more capable in the world (Learmonth, Cuevas, & Rovee-Collier, 2015). Some theoretical accounts of infant memory and infantile amnesia place procedural memory at the center of the types of memory infants can show, claiming that most if not all infant memories are implicit (Rovee-Collier, 1997).

This, however, is a hotly debated point. For the purposes of this discussion it is clear that as soon as infants can show voluntary control over their bodily movements they can develop procedural memories and behavioral habits like the rest of us. As stated previously, procedural memory allows for the execution of actions without adding to the cognitive load and thus would be important to everyday functioning in an infant.

Implicit Memory Sub-types

In addition to being broadly differentiated from explicit memory, implicit memory has several dissociable subtypes, perceptual and conceptual as well as emotional and affective. Perceptual implicit memory allows for the completion of fragmented and blurry images, while conceptual implicit memory facilitates connections between related, but perceptually different forms (e.g., a faster response to the word dog after being primed with the word puppy). Findings from affective and emotive memory suggest that previous emotional experiences can color a current experience's emotional valence and arousal properties. Implicit memory includes a number of different types of phenomena discussed in depth later in this volume.

Just a few of the ways in which implicit memory is manifested include priming (defined as an unconscious effect of previous exposure in the classification, identification and production of information), procedural memory (which is memory for an action sequence that is not part of a conscious process; the difficulty explaining how to drive or ride a bicycle to a novice makes obvious how those action sequences are not easily available to conscious examination). Individuals show a preference for the familiarity fostered by a melody previously heard but not explicitly remembered. Prior exposure to letter fonts promotes faster decoding and more fluent reading of those fonts when lettering is disrupted.

Studies of neural systems using a number of neuroimaging techniques also provide evidence differentiating implicit memory from explicit memory. When we are consciously recalling a memory, activity is increased in the prefrontal cortex as well as the hippocampus and medial temporal lobe. This set of activations is not associated with implicit memory. That is, implicit systems seem to function in a couple of different ways. Evidence from both imaging and ERP techniques suggest that priming reduces activity in the brain areas associated with the task. The reduction seems to be associated with the demands of the task, such that tasks with a perceptual component (word-stem, fragment completion, blurry picture identification) are associated with decreased activity in the visual cortex (Schacter, 2019; Squire, 2004).

When the task is more conceptual, the decreased activity is found in the inferior frontal and mid-temporal areas (Carlesimo et al., 1996). One explanation offered for this decrease in activity is that the neural substrates used for the initial processing of the information are engaged to reprocess the information and are showing a decrease in activity because the information has been processed before and that repeated processing reduces activity demands (Koutstaal, Wagner, Rotte, Maril, Buckner & Schacter, 2001). Put simply, it is easier to reprocess an item than to process it the first time and many activities completed within the implicit memory systems are familiar, often repeated activities.

Clearly, memories below the level of conscious awareness, and revealed through implicit techniques, exert a significant impact on the way we live our lives.

Procedural Memory

Procedural memory is memory for how to do something (Squire, 1987). It has sometimes been characterized as habit memory or memory for skills and habits. It is the kind of memory that allows us to open a jar without spending time or resources figuring out which way to turn the lid, and why when something screws in the wrong direction we have difficulty with it every time. Rarely does the right way to unscrew the top of the jar enter our consciousness, instead we are consciously thinking about the contents of the jar and our current use of the contents. Procedural memory allows us to complete a familiar action without it adding to our cognitive load, without having to invest willful conscious effort (Harrington, Haaland, Yeo & Marder, 2008).

Not having to think about how my feet need to move while I am running frees up resources to look at the scenery or avoid cars. In everyday life there are a huge number of procedural memories that we use to make complex tasks less demanding of attention and conscious resources. This lower demand provided by a practiced skill allows our conscious attention to be allocated to something other than the physical skills necessary to, for example, type on my keyboard. If I could type well enough to do it without looking at the keys, I would be a much faster writer.

Much of the information we have about procedural memory indicates that the things we do using procedural memory are practiced skills that become second nature and implicit, requiring little or no conscious effort. Over time many routine tasks that started out as difficult and requiring many resources become overlearned and automatic (Harrington, Haaland, Yeo & Marder, 2008). Watching a child on a two-wheeled bicycle for the first time is a study in the difficulty of balancing on the wheels, pumping the pedals and steering, simultaneously. Early in the learning process, it takes all of the child's resources to stay on the bicycle and remain upright, and sometimes it is not enough. A few short months later and after a lot of practice, the same child who was struggling to manage those multiple difficult tasks is lifting (preferably just one) a hand to wave as she rides by, with no apparent effort.

Over time and practice, a skill that started out as difficult and demanding of many cognitive resources becomes a procedural memory skill and no longer requires the same investment of resources, once again allowing the individual to direct their cognitive resources to some other tasks while they execute the familiar procedural task. Importantly, new procedural tasks that contain elements of previously learned tasks are learned more quickly and efficiently, indicating that existing procedural memories influence the creation of new procedural memories (King, Dolfen, Gann, Renard, Swinnen, & Albouy, 2019). Procedural memories are difficult to bring into conscious recollection as the context for their creation largely remains unavailable to recollection (this is why it can be so difficult to teach someone else to ride a bike or drive a car).

Procedural Memories and Neurologic Injury

Access to these memories, in the absence of awareness, offers a window into prior learning and memory, in the face of brain injury. That is, procedural memory is relatively preserved in patients with various types of brain damage, indicating that the neural systems that underlie other types of memory may not the same as the systems that underlie procedural memory. For example, patients with amnesia and with Parkinson's disease have been shown to have preserved procedural memory (Knowlton, Mangels & Squire, 1996). This may suggest that damage associated with compromised explicit and conscious memory systems and that may also be compromised in some neurodegenerative disorders may not impact procedural memory.

However, there is some recent evidence that in sequence learning, the hippocampus, which is important to conscious memory, could be involved with procedural memory at least some of the time (King et al., 2019). This could mean that procedural memories can be formed in multiple ways or that the hippocampus can be recruited by the procedural memory system in some situations. Procedural memory does not require awareness, meaning that the patients who show procedural memory for a task may report no conscious memory of the task or may even state that they do not know how to complete the task (Squire, 2004; Smith et al., 2014).

Research has shown that the critical brain regions involved in procedural memory are in the striatum with some work specifically indicating the neostriatum (Ferbinteanu, 2018) and the dorsal striatum (Packard & McGaugh, 1992), indicating that these regions are in a different part of the brain than conscious memory. Multiple studies of patients with amnesia of different types, starting with H.M., show that procedural memory is preserved even when conscious memory is severely compromised, completely nonexistent or inaccessible (Cohen & Squire, 1980).

Priming

Priming represents the effect of previous exposure to a stimulus whereby it influences the classification, identification and production of information. It is unconscious, effortless and automatic and can influence behavior in a wide variety of timeframes, with effects that can last from milliseconds to years depending on the situation and stimuli (Was, Woltz & Hirsch, 2019). Priming as a method of showing implicit effects has a long history. In fact, some discussions of implicit memory focus almost entirely on priming as the mechanism to reveal implicit knowledge (Bowers & Marsolek, 2003). Priming protocols are often used in experimental situations because it is easy to use experimentally and easy to manipulate with respect to the different types of information that can be used in this implicit task. Although there are hints that some philosophers whose word was foundational to modern psychology were aware of some of the types of priming, the systematic study of priming began in the late 1960s and early 1970s (Schacter, 1987). The early studies of priming used a technique that required participants to complete word fragments and identify picture fragments (Warrington & Weiskrantz, 1970).

In the following decades, studies that use priming have become more variable and complex. Evidence that semantic priming is task dependent (de Wit & Kinoshita, 2015) and influenced by the memory load in a task (Heyman, Van Rensbergen, Storms, Hutchison, & De Deyne, 2015) indicates that semantic priming comes in multiple forms and features of the task should be considered when evaluating priming research.

People show priming effects across a wide variety of situations and tasks. There is evidence that priming influences conscious memory as well as behavior though the priming itself is unconscious (Park & Donaldson, 2016). The results of numerous tasks have substantiated that previous exposure to words, pictures, and other stimuli influence the speed with which these items are identified and classified (Schendan, 2017). In everyday life, priming has a big influence on the words we choose to express a thought and the speed and accuracy with which we identify and classify everyday items in our lives. Research shows that people fill in a word stem with words that were in a previous study session even if they do not consciously recall the words from that list (Craik, Rose & Gopie, 2015).

The focus of priming research has often been words or pictures, but in social psychology there is also a literature that focuses on how priming effects influence our social behavior, even though those effects are not at the level of consciousness (Doyen, Klein, Simons & Cleeremans, 2014). For example, in an ambiguous situation, such as walking down a dark street, the sight of another walker can be threatening or reassuring depending on aspects of the place and the walker's recent experience. In that moment, the walker is not thinking about what aspects of the situation determine the interpretation of events, instead they are responding to the signals of the situation that elicit a primed response.

Priming can be perceptual, conceptual or semantic with repetition priming as a special case of perceptual or conceptual priming. Perceptual priming relies on how the stimuli look and can be seen in things like greater priming for words presented in the same font over words that have font or case changes in the letters, even though in all cases it is the same word. Perceptual priming also allows people to identify blurred pictures they have seen before faster and more accurately than novel pictures, this effect can be found in adults and preschool children (Drummey & Newcombe, 1995; Burgund, Marsolek & Luciana, 2003). Conceptual priming happens when the perceptual features of the stimuli do change from one presentation to another, meaning the perceptual process is no longer available, but priming can still be seen, albeit at lower levels. For example, participants are faster to respond to another dog over a cat or giraffe if they have been primed with a dog (Was, Woltz & Hirsch, 2018).

Semantic priming is considered a special case of conceptual priming and has often, but not always, been found to be more ephemeral, lasting only a second in most cases. Semantic priming is when some aspect of the meaning of the first word is related to the next word and response times decrease and accuracy increases. It is the basis of many word association games. Despite the fact that both conceptual and perceptual priming are referred to as priming, these two types of priming are most often considered to be distinct forms of memory. Repetition priming has also been proposed to be a distinct category of learning, operating at the perceptual, pre-semantic level (Tulving & Schacter, 1990). Repetition priming is the effect of repeated exposure and it can be either perceptual or conceptual. In real life this is often when in the middle of a conversation one becomes aware that they have repeated the same phrasing their conversational partner used a moment ago.

Situational factors are important in priming. Changes in different aspects of the primed stimulus influence the strength of the primed response. Meaningful stimuli show bigger priming effects (Kiefer, 2002). For example, tasks using words evoke better priming than tasks using nonsense syllables, so it is easier to prime a study participant with apple than appne. Tasks that are presented within a single sensory modality, both stimuli at presentation and at testing, yield larger priming effects versus mixed modality scenarios (i.e., visually at familiarization and auditory at test) (Schendan, 2017). Moreover, experimental studies show that different task elements differentially affect priming versus explicit memory (Parker, Powell, & Dagnall, 2018).

Priming is likely to be associated with some type of resource conservation. In other words, brain activity has been shown to be reduced for objects that are primed, in addition responding is faster and more accurate than on new tasks (Koutstaal, Wagner, Rotte, Maril, Buckner & Schacter, 2001). Why does all of this matter and what does it have to do with the world of unaware memory? The answer is found in the fact that priming, which has a distinct neural signature, is often preserved in patients with brain damage that interferes with their ability to access explicit memory (Schacter, Dobbins & Schnyer, 2004). Patients with medial temporal lobe amnesia show priming effects even when they have no conscious memory of the events. Participants without brain damage do not need to have conscious memory for previous events in order to show priming (Schendan, 2017).

Importantly, priming does not rely on the temporal lobe (Schacter, Dobbins & Schnyer, 2004) which is so important for conscious or explicit memory. However, there is some evidence that priming and the conscious experience of familiarity have overlapping neural signatures (Kinoshita, 2003; Thakral, Kensinger & Slotnick, 2016)

Preservation of Priming

Research that started with H.M. and eventually included a number of patients with temporal lobe damage showed that although most patients showed a severely impaired or a total inability to form new conscious memories, their ability to show priming was generally preserved. The preservation of priming in these patients suggests that it is not mediated through the temporal lobe, with research implicating the neocortex (Squire, 2004). In other words, the window to the world of unaware memory appears to be expressed through priming.

Priming: A developmental perspective

Interestingly, priming is available from very early in life and can be seen in babies by three months. It is possible babies show priming earlier, but measuring it earlier is difficult. Infants at three months and possibly younger show priming effects in a number of operant tasks (Rovee-Collier et al., 2002). In both infants and adults priming is very specific. That is, in infants changing any element of a primed item, in a task that is similar to repetition priming in older participants, inhibits their performance. For example, changing one element in a mobile or a colorful crib liner that is not task relevant interferes with the infants' priming (Rovee-Collier & Cuevas, 2008). While adults show greater flexibility then infants, priming is also described in adults as hyper specific (Tulving & Schacter, 1990).

Priming: Lexical and Semantic

Lexical and semantic priming are two of the most common forms of priming used in laboratory studies and as such, they have been a part of research into implicit memory from its early beginnings. In the early stages of research into implicit processes, the terms priming, and implicit memory were sometimes used interchangeably, but as research found additional types implicit learning and memory, priming became just one component of implicit phenomena.

The procedures for lexical and semantic priming studies, in general, include exposing the participants to words that can be masked or exposed very briefly followed by a test that requires participants to show the effect of the prime by faster or more accurate responding to test stimuli that are activated by the prime. At test, participants are more likely to fill out a word-stem completion or a semantic prompt with words that are primed. Results show that the primed words are more likely to be produced in answer to the prompt even if there are other words that would fit and are of equal or greater frequency in language use.

Priming studies show that previously exposed stimuli are more likely to be retrieved at test even if the participants do not explicitly remember the previously exposed stimuli. Lexical and semantic priming take advantage of the form and meaning of words used as the prime. In lexical priming, the word or words that are primed are later identified by the study participant sometimes as a word or a pseudoword and other times same or different from the primed word or words at test.

For example, Lee and Zhang (2018) asked participants to differentiate between target words followed by another word or a pronounceable pseudoword. Participants responded by pressing word or non-word buttons on a keyboard. Scoring measured accuracy and response time. In semantic priming the meaning of the prime influences test performance. Participants respond faster and more accurately if a word at test is related to the primed word or the primed word makes it more likely for the participant to use a related word.

Therefore, participants primed with prince, answer the prompt "female royalty" with princess more often than unprimed participants. Participants are also faster to identify a related word when asked to differentiate words from pseudowords or different types of words (Lee & Zhang, 2017). For example, participants identify dog or cat as animals when they follow the prime pets than when they follow the prime spiders. Semantic priming can be positive, increasing the likelihood of a response to the primed target, or negative, decreasing the likelihood of a response to the primed target. Priming tasks that are used in research vary widely so the previous examples constitute a random sample of the wide range of possibilities.

Neurologic Disorders and Priming

As with other implicit tasks, both semantic and lexical priming are preserved, or somewhat preserved in cases of neurological diseases that compromise conscious memory. In the case of semantic priming, patients with transient global amnesia, characterized by a profound anterograde amnesia, showed priming effects in a semantic priming task that persisted for at least one day (Guillery, Desgranges, Katis, Viader, & Eustache, 2001). Studies of the impact of Alzheimer's disease on semantic priming showed great variability in whether word-stem completion priming was intact or impaired. Salmon and Heindel (2014) argue that priming in patients with Alzheimer's disease may depend upon the integrity of semantic and lexical representations.

Research has used semantic priming tasks to suggest that the integrity of semantic processing may be compromised in Parkinson's disease (Angwin, Chenery, Copland, Murdoch, & Silburn, 2005; Arnott, Chenery, Murdoch, & Silburn, 2001).There are significantly different patterns of semantic priming for the Parkinson's disease patients as compared to healthy older adults.

In the case of lexical priming, Parkinson's disease patients displayed hyper identity priming relative to controls (Filoteo et al., 2003). In a word/nonword paradigm, lexical priming findings suggest that the speed of lexical access may be compromised in Parkinson's disease (Angwin, Chenery, Copland, Murdoch, & Silburn, 2007). As the aforementioned studies demonstrate, priming tasks can be used to examine what kinds of issues underlie the memory deficits in a large number of disorders.

Priming can also be used with children to explore their understanding of written text. For example, children with dyslexia exhibit enhanced semantic processing during reading which may reflect a compensatory mechanism for deficient phonological processing. An interesting study recently showed that in contrast to the phonological condition, the semantic condition showed priming effects that were, in fact, stronger in children with dyslexia than in typical readers. This lead to the conclusion that children with dyslexia, compared with typical readers, rely more on semantic information in word reading but do not show deficient phonological activation during reading compared with typical readers.

Individual word and pseudoword reading efficiency correlated with priming effects only in the semantic condition and only in children with dyslexia (Van der Kleij, Groen, Segers, & Verhoeven, 2019). In these examples, priming techniques can be used to parse the compensatory strategies of children for whom reading is particularly difficult.

As the example of children with dyslexia having stronger semantic priming shows, in everyday life priming effects can be helpful when compensating for a disability or completing a difficult task. In other words, the world of unaware phenomena, in the form of priming is a part of everyday functioning. When we step into our homes or offices there are priming effects that influence how quickly and accurately, we respond to home and business-related issues. Priming is more efficient when it occurs in the original context in which the priming was established. So, we can address a business-related matter when sitting on the couch at home, but our responses are likely to be both faster and more accurate at the business site when the business context primes the response.

Chapter 2

Familiarity and Priming

FAMILIARITY PREFERENCE

Familiarity preference is a tendency for people to show a preference for stimuli they have encountered previously (although do not explicitly remember) over novel or unfamiliar stimuli. There are a large number of ways that familiarity preferences can be assessed, most of which are related to speed of processing familiar information. In adults, participants are presented with stimuli, usually in the form of pictures or words. At a later test, participants tend to show a preference for these words or pictures even if they cannot consciously remember them from the earlier presentation (Diamond, Mayes & Meudell, 2011). The area where familiarity preference is used in ways that revolutionized what we know about cognition is in infancy.

Researchers have used the familiarly preference phenomenon to show that infants who are too young to show many behavioral responses other than looking at stimuli presented to them have the same kind of preference for familiarly as older humans. Accessing this familiarity preference in infants is generally done in a looking paradigm where the infant has the opportunity to look at two different images. Infants show that they can remember and prefer previously exposed items in the differential patterns with which they look at familiar as compared to novel stimuli.

There are a number of ways to see familiarity preferences in healthy adults as well as children. Two of the most commonly studied areas are sound and food preferences. Familiarity of the taste of a food is an important factor when assessing consumer preferences (Lahne, Trubek, & Pelchat, 2014). And recent research has shown that adult participants who, while not music experts, prefer both musicians and songs that are familiar over unfamiliar music, while the expert raters were not influenced by familiarity (Lundy, Allred, & Peebles, 2019).

Familiarity plays an important role in preferences for a large array of stimuli. Responses to familiar stimuli are faster than those to unfamiliar stimuli. Models of the structure of memory indicate that recognition of familiar stimuli is fast and automatic, while other types of memory, most of which are conscious, take more time and effort to process (Brainerd, Nakamura, & Lee, 2019).

Familiar stimuli do not require the same amount of processing as unfamiliar stimuli, thus familiar stimuli are easier and require fewer cognitive resources to process (Kahneman, 2011). According to Kahneman (2011), cognitive ease is one of the ways we make decisions about information and that ease is created by familiarity. Therefore, even if we do not explicitly remember information, that sense of familiarity can and does influence our decision-making, often operating on an unaware level.

Familiarity and Neurodegenerative Disease

In people with neurodegenerative disease, familiarity can be very important. Patients with amnesia and mild cognitive impairment can perform similarly to healthy controls in a task that assesses familiarity, while having difficulty on recollection tasks (Besson, Ceccaldi, Tramoni, Felician, Didic, & Barbeau, 2015). Koen and Yonelinas (2014) conducted a meta-analysis that showed that healthy older adults show declines in recollection, but not in familiarity and patients with amnesia and mild cognitive impairment have a preserved sense of familiarity, while patients with Alzheimer's disease showed declines in both familiarity and recollection.

In a similar vein, people with mild cognitive impairments can function better and prefer familiar environments (Gold, Park, Murphy, & Troyer, 2015). For example, patients with mild cognitive impairment who live in the house they lived in for years can rely on their familiarity of that house to allow better functioning than if they moved to a new living arrangement. Mild cognitive impairment is often the precursor to Alzheimer's disease where familiarity is impaired as well as recollection (Koen & Yonelinas 2014). Familiarity can also be helpful for patients who have suffered damage to their explicit memory systems because the familiarity preference is still available to them and familiar settings and stimuli can be helpful in facilitating their everyday functioning.

Familiarity in Infants

In infants, the preference for familiar stimuli has been used to explore a large number of important areas of infant cognition, including how long infants remember an item and how their memory changes over the course of the first few years of life (Rovee-Collier, Hayne & Colombo, 2001). Information that cannot be retrieved in explicit ways can be indicated via preference. That is, infants' preference for familiarity provides a way to access the knowledge and memory of infants who are too young and physically limited to do anything other than look at objects or kick mobiles (Rovee-Collier, Hayne & Colombo, 2001).

Young children show strong preferences for familiar stimuli and familiar situations as any parent of a toddler will tell you about the notorious preference for familiar toys and foods. Children on the autism spectrum show an even greater preference for familiarity and can struggle with even minor changes to their routine (Kenzer & Bishop, 2011). Something as simple as their school bus being detoured on the way to school can cause these children intense distress.

Familiarity Preference and Everyday Life

The preference for familiarity can be shown in laboratory studies, but it can also be shown in everyday activities. For most people, it is not an unfamiliar experience to discover that they strongly prefer the way they have been doing an activity, which can explain why it takes time for new procedures to take hold in an organization. Even if the new way of doing things is more efficient or has some distinct advantage over the old, there is a tendency for people to prefer the familiar old way of doing things. This slow adaptation to new routines and procedures reflects a familiarity preference. In everyday life, a familiarity preference can be expressed as a preference for stimuli and routines that can be executed with fewer cognitive resources than it takes to process and think about more novel stimuli and routines (Hsin-I, Su-Ling, Shinsuke, 2011).

The preference for familiarity is a way to reduce the amount of resources needed for almost any activity. Recruitment of procedural memory and priming reflects a preference for ways to engage in everyday activities without placing great demands on processing resources, thus freeing cognitive resources for tasks that cannot be automatized because they are new, or they require the kind of attention that only consciously-mediated phenomena can recruit.

Real-World Implications of Priming: An Integration

Does automatic access to memories have real-world implications? The answer lies in the fact that priming is an important part of everyday functioning. This is so, because the speed and automaticity of priming frees resources for other tasks, while allowing an individual to respond appropriately when confronted with familiar stimuli. The primed behavior is more efficient than a behavior that is not primed. The world of unaware memories can also impact explicit recognition producing changes in the speed with which information is retrieved, as well as producing changes in the onset and duration of memory effects. Thus, priming while playing a role in unaware memory has also been found to increase the processing speed of conscious explicit memory (Park & Donaldson, 2016).

Chapter 3

Emotions, Valence and Arousal

Any discussion of emotional memory should provide some insight into what emotions are and how they work. Emotions can be categorized along two orthogonal dimensions, valence and arousal (Barrett, 2017; LeDoux, 2014). Valence refers to the status of the emotional response from positive to negative. This dimension is the one most often discussed in subjective discussions of emotion, with happiness and sadness differentiated along with ennui and anger.

Arousal refers to the level of physiological response that accompanies the emotion. Low arousal emotions can be manifested as ennui and satisfaction, while high arousal emotions can be manifested as anger and joy, but these examples are limited because even anger and joy can have both low energy (low arousal) and high energy (high arousal) forms. Why this information is important to emotional memory is that the emotional memories that influence human thought and behavior can vary along both of these dimensions.

The complexity of the different combinations of valence and arousal is enormous and results in the rich and varied emotional lives humans live. Valence and arousal are dimensions of emotional responses that differentially affect memory and behavior. Much of the research in this area has been done looking at fear. One reason for this is that the fear response in rodent models has a long research history and another because fear is a symptom that is manifested in a variety of clinical disorders and it is difficult to process and identify in certain neurodevelopmental disorders.

The mechanisms that underlie emotions are poorly understood and difficult to measure directly but instead must be measured as an indirect expression (LeDoux, 2012). It is clear that emotion plays a role in both conscious and unconscious memory. Although not reporting any conscious emotion, humans can, nevertheless, respond to threatening stimuli without showing markers of being aware of the relevant stimulus (LeDoux, 2014).

Barrett (2016) offers a more holistic view that has emotional context influencing all of our thoughts and behaviors and that our initial response is along the two major dimensions of valence and arousal. The response is then inter-preted using our current state and previous experience to evoke the emotion we feel. This view has consequences for the world of unaware memory as emotional memories can impact decisions and behaviors on an unaware level even when we are consciously trying to be objective (Barrett, 2016).

Emotional stimuli, particularly those associated with fear, trigger survival circuits that result in responses intended to protect the organism from harm or mitigate that harm as much as possible. These emotions are integrated with the survival circuits and compared to similar states in long-term memory which can generate an emotional state that can trigger protective and avoidant behaviors (LeDoux, 2012). These states can be perceived at a conscious level, but can also fall below the level of consciousness, but in either case they can influence behavior, both in the moment and beyond the immediate context.

EMOTION AND BRAIN

Affective and emotive memories are represented in distinct brain regions compared to other types of memory. Research derived from multiple studies suggests that the amygdala, particularly the basolateral amygdala, has been implicated in affective memory. Studies using both human and rodent mod-els have found double dissociations between affective memories and either declarative or procedural memories (Bechara, Tranel, Damasio & Adolphs, 1995; McDonald & Hong, 2004).

What this means is that disrupting the animal's ability to form conscious memories and learn new skills has no effect on emotional memory and dis-rupting emotional memory has no effect on conscious memory formation or skill learning. Emotional arousal associated with stress and anxiety can bias responses in both human and animal models in the direction of relying more on habit than declarative memory in a number of different memory dependent tasks (Packard & Goodman, 2012). These studies indicate that emotional arousal is an integral part of memory formation for emotional events, but it also appears to influence which type of memory is recruited in response to task demands or to solve a problem.

The tendency to rely on habit means that under conditions of stress, prob-lem solving will be less responsive to situational variables and less creative. This research places emotion and the basolateral amygdala as important modulators of memory processes that can result in both enhancement or impairment depending on stress or emotional arousal context (Packard & Goodman, 2012).

Thus, in our everyday life, emotional memory can influence how we experience new events with the processes mediating these associations often operating on an unconscious level. Taken together, these findings add an additional nuance to our understanding of how the world of unaware memories and their associated valence and arousal levels can influence how we process and respond to stimuli, situations and events.

Emotive Memory

Thus the world of unaware memory is also inhabited by emotional memory, which is a special category of memory that is important for learning and storing information about the emotional significance of events. This kind of memory is implicit and so unavailable to conscious access (LeDoux, 1993). Emotional memory can relate to the emotions attached to specific things (specific cues for that emotion) or about the emotional significance of contextual information which is more general and does not relate to specific objects or sensory cues.

For example, emotional memories can be tied to a specific object or event (i.e., baking cookies with your daughter which brings you back in time to that sense of belonging and connection you had with your grandmother who taught you how to bake) and to specific contextual information (walking into a classroom to give an exam elicits echoes of the anxiety you may have felt as a student preparing to take an exam). These two ways in which emotional memory influence behavior are often, but may not necessarily, always be below the level of consciousness (Hine & Tsushima, 2018).

For example, you might think about your anxiety when walking into a classroom when there is a test, but more often, you just feel the rise in anxiety without conscious memory for why or how it came about.

Chapter 4

Perceptual Processing, Procedural Learning and Language

PERCEPTUAL PROCESSING, PROCEDURAL LEARNING AND UNAWARENESS: MIRRORING MEMORY

Reading script that has been inverted and reflected in a mirror is one of the methods that have been used to see how people learn how to adapt to reading familiar stimuli presented in an unfamiliar form. This adaptation is a type of perceptual procedural learning in which people become better at performing the task with practice. Much like the motor examples of procedural learning, reading mirrored and inverted script improves predictably with practice and can become a skill that requires little conscious effort once it becomes a practiced skill. For most participants, there is an adaption period when they have difficulty reading the text, but over time and with practice, people show a steady learning curve and can with significant practice learn to read the mirror inverted script fluidly. Acquisition is usually measured as increased accuracy and speed that is dependent on repeated exposure to reflected inverted written text. Participants who have learned to read mirror inverted script retain this type of learning for a relatively long period of time, at least a few weeks (Dirnberger & Novak-Knollmueller, 2013), and longer with continued practice.

This is an example of procedural learning that does not include a motor component. In typically functioning adults, learning to read mirror-inverted text is closely related, but not identical, to learning motor procedural tasks. Dirnberger and Novak-Knollmueller (2013) measured mirror-inverted text reading among other procedural tasks that had a motor component, in a sample of healthy adult participants. They found that reading mirror reflected inverted text demonstrated that participants learn to read the text in a pattern that is similar to the learning curves for other procedural tasks and that the learning is retained for a relatively long time.

They interpreted this positive correlation between motor and perceptual learning as suggesting that the motor and perceptual procedural learning mechanisms act in parallel and are not opposing or competing processes. More evidence that the perceptual and motor procedural memory systems are complementary comes from the finding that the speed of learning to read mirror-inverted script was related to speed differentials between the right and left hand on a simple motor task in young adults (Annett, 1991).

These findings indicate that there is a relationship between motor performance and learning to read mirror-inverted script and that this relationship makes mirror-inverted text reading a good task for assessment of procedural learning with populations that might have difficulty with procedural learning that requires a motor response.

So, what does all of this have to do with the world of unaware memory? Simply put, patients with amnesia show preserved learning in mirror learning tasks. In other words, despite the fact that amnesics do not remember having previously been exposed to reading mirror-inverted script, they nevertheless do show evidence of learning as manifested by improved performance reading inverted script versus baseline performance.

In fact, Cohen and Squire (1980) demonstrated that amnesic patients showed learning that was comparable to healthy matched controls at mirror reading skill, including improvement over multiple sessions, indicating savings from one session to the next. That said, the amnesic patients had no recall of their prior training experience.

Mirror Reading in Clinical Populations

Differentiating perceptual from motor procedural learning allows researchers to observe procedural learning in patients with neurological or physical constraints that interfere with motor performance. For example, patients with Parkinson's disease can have difficulty with procedural memory tasks that require movement of pieces or other motor responses (Harrington, Haaland, Yeo & Marder, 1990), but show intact performance for reading mirror-inverted text, as long as the words were repeated in the procedure and target tracking (Koenig, Thomas-Antérion & Laurent, 1999). There is also evidence that patients with Parkinson's disease show deficits in short-term retention of both motor and perceptual procedural skill learning compared to healthy adults (Koenig et al., 1999).

However, some recent research shows that in reading mirror-inverted text, patients with Parkinson's disease were not different from a healthy older adult control group on either acquisition or retention (Panouillères, Tofaris, Brown

& Jenkinson, 2016). This relatively intact procedural learning for tasks that do not have a motor component is important to understanding the difficulties Parkinson's patients face with some difficulties masked or exaggerated by symptoms inherent in the disease.

Patients with Alzheimer's disease do not show recall for the information in the text, but do show increases in speed and accuracy of reading mirror-inverted script over repeated trials (Bondi & Kaszniak, 1991). Different from Parkinson's and Alzheimer's diseases, patients with cerebellar stroke showed learning in a motor procedural task, but not in mirror inverted text reading, indicating the importance of the cerebellum to performance on the perceptually based task but not the motor-based tasks (Dirnberger, Novak & Nasel, 2013).

Vakil and Galon (2014) report that the learning rate for patients with a traumatic brain injury (TBI) was preserved but the response time of the group with TBI was slower than that of healthy controls. Patients with schizophrenia show slower learning, but there is some evidence that this could be related to the medications used to manage the symptoms instead of the disorder itself (Rémillard, Pourcher & Cohen, 2010).

Mirror-Inverted Script and Children

The development of the ability to read mirror inverted script can be seen in some research done with school-age children. The findings were that children who were good readers show slower but substantially similar learning curves as college undergraduates (Annett, 1991). One motivation for this research into mirror inverted reading was the finding that young children confuse mirror letters, such as b and d frequently as they are learning to read. Recent studies show that children make mirror errors because they overgeneralize the shape of the letters, mirror inverted or not (Ahr, Houdé & Borst, 2016).

Everyday Applications

Reading mirrored and inverted script in everyday life is not usually a skill that people practice, however, it is a combination of two skills many people use regularly. Being able to read text upside down can make riding on the subway more interesting or make it possible to see that the person you are meeting with has the wrong report in front of them. Additionally, glass doors with text on the other side can provide a need to read mirrored, but not inverted text. However, there is evidence that people navigating the everyday world have significant difficulty with instructions on the other side of a glass door, probably because if you decode that the word on the other side of the glass is "push," you actually need to pull that door open from your side (Boldt, Stürmer, Gaschler, Schacht & Sommer, 2013).

Perceptual Implicit Memory: Modality Effects

The sensory modality (auditory, visual, haptic, smell, taste) with which information is presented has an effect on how that information is recalled and used in humans. Perceptual implicit memory is typically most robust when the perceptual processing at encoding matches the perceptual processing required during retrieval (Mulligan, 2011). Furthermore, there is evidence that the effect of modality is stronger for implicit tasks than explicit ones (Schacter & Graf, 1989). In general, the way that modality effects are tested in the laboratory is that participants are presented with information or form associations between pieces of information in one modality and tested in that same modality as well as alternative modalities.

For example, participants could be presented with pairs of unrelated words to form associations in written text that they were given to study. At test, the participants are presented with some of the study words in written form and others aurally. The words presented in the same form as they were studied will be more likely to be reproduced in an implicit task indicating an effect of modality. Verbalizing our understanding of how implicit phenomena are facilitated is important but difficult given that so much learning happens in an implicit fashion and happens unintentionally and automatically.

An important goal of the research into modality specificity is to establish whether implicit learning is underwritten by a single, domain-general mechanism that applies across a wide range of tasks, input, and domains, or instead consists of multiple tasks or stimulus-specific subsystems. Implicit learning has been demonstrated across multiple input types and different tasks, but that does not necessarily imply a single, domain-general system. It is also possible that there are multiple implicit learning systems or subsystems that all have similar features, but are only engaged for specific tasks and input demands.

Some of the early studies that showed modality specificity were described as creating a theoretical puzzle because they indicated that within implicit memory, "access to the products of elaborative processing depends on modality-specific, sensory-perceptual processing" (Schacter & Graf, 1989, pg. 3). These first studies were followed by a large number of studies using different techniques to examine modality effects.

Several studies used correlational analyses to suggest that implicit learning is relatively task-specific (Feldman, Kerr, & Streissguth, 1995; Gebauer & Mackintosh, 2007). One of the experimental studies that addressed three different modalities was Conway and Christianson (2005), who tested sequence learning in the visual, auditory, and tactile modalities. They presented participants with sequences that were visual, squares in different locations, auditory, multiple tones in sequences, and tactile pulses delivered to the fingers. They tested the participants' ability to correctly classify novel sequences as being generated from the same grammar pattern.

They found that visual learning performance was nearly identical to tactile learning, but auditory learning scores were much higher than either tactile or visual learning. In this task, they found that auditory implicit learning was more efficient than both tactile and visual learning. So not only is there an advantage to being tested in the same modality as learning occurred, but also there are differences in learning rates between different modalities.

They claim that their findings indicate that not only does auditory implicit learning have an advantage over tactile and visual learning, but also that there may be differences in implicit learning between the three modalities. Tactile learning may be more sensitive to statistical structure at the beginnings of the sequences while auditory learning may be more sensitive to the structure at the end of the sequence. They suggest that these findings could imply that each sensory system may use different computational strategies when processing sequential information (Conway & Christianson, 2005).

Chapter 5

Cross-Modality Effects

Another important feature of modality in implicit learning and memory is cross-modal priming where people show effects of implicit learning and memory when they are tested in a different modality. The implicit effects are generally but not always smaller than effects that are tested in the same modality, but they are reliable. Many of the cross-modal implicit learning studies show a cross-modal implicit learning effect that suggests that information can be processed in a cross-modal representation without conscious processing (Taesler, Jablonowski, Fu, & Rose, 2019).

Multiple studies show these effects across different modalities. For example, using visual information to prime an auditory task and vice versa (Walk & Conway, 2016), tactile stimulation to prime a spatial auditory task (Tonelli, Gori, & Brayda, 2016), all involving crossing modalities and using different protocols with widely variable task demands.

These findings are relevant to the theme of this volume, as they provide additional evidence showing that it is possible to use information that is below the level of conscious awareness and across modalities to impact behavior.

Patients with Alzheimer's disease are thought to have mostly intact implicit functioning showing both cross modal and within modality priming readily (Carlesimo, Mauri, Fadda, Turriziani & Caltagirone, 2001). Even though most of the implicit systems seem to be preserved in Alzheimer's, there are studies demonstrating that although Alzheimer's patients have preserved cross modal priming in perceptual tasks, that preservation may not extend to conceptual implicit tasks (Vallet et al., 2013).

The learning rates over time differed for both modality and the stimuli within modalities, although there was no correlation to global error rates or reaction time differences between the stimulus types. These results demonstrate a modeling method that is well suited to extract detailed information about the success of implicit learning from high variability data. It further shows a cross-modal implicit learning effect which extends our understanding of implicit learning systems and provides additional support for the idea that information can be processed in a cross-modal representation without being mediated by conscious processing (Taesler, Jablonowski, Fu, & Rose, 2019).

Cognitive maps elicited by touch may participate in cross-modal calibration and supra-modal representations of space that increase implicit knowledge about sound propagation (Tonelli, Gori, & Brayda, 2016). Recent studies have demonstrated participants' ability to learn cross-modal associations during statistical learning tasks. However, these studies are all similar in that the cross-modal associations to be learned occur simultaneously, rather than sequentially. In addition, the majority of these studies focused on learning across sensory modalities but not across perceptual categories.

To test both cross-modal and cross-categorical learning of sequential dependencies, an artificial grammar learning task consisting of a serial stream of auditory and/or visual stimuli containing both within- and cross-domain dependencies was used. Experiment 1 examined within-modal and cross-modal learning across two sensory modalities (audition and vision). Experiment 2 investigated within-categorical and cross-categorical learning across two perceptual categories within the same sensory modality (e.g., shape and color; tones and non-words). The results indicated that individuals demonstrated learning of the within-modal and within-categorical but not the cross-modal or cross-categorical dependencies. These results stand in contrast to the previous demonstrations of cross-modal statistical learning, and highlight the presence of modality constraints that limit the effectiveness of learning in a multimodal environment (Walk & Conway, 2016).

As previously noted, priming is an implicit memory effect in which previous exposure to one stimulus influences the response to another stimulus. A key characteristic of priming is that it occurs without awareness and can take place even when the physical attributes of previously studied and test stimuli do not match.

CROSS MODAL EFFECTS: PHYSIOLOGICAL CORRELATES

Relatedly, Sebastiani et al. (2015), using a cross modal word-stem completion task explored the mechanisms underlying negative priming scores and the putative role played by inefficient word processing at study altering stimulus representation. In this protocol, words were presented in the auditory modality and word-stem completions were to be completed in the visual modality. At study, the authors recorded auditory ERPs, and compared the P300 (attention/memory) and N400 (meaning processing) of individuals who exhibited positive and negative priming. Besides classical averaging-based

ERP analysis, an ICA-based method (ErpICASSO) was used to separate the potentials related to different processes contributing to ERPs.

Classical analysis yielded significant differences between the two waves across the whole scalp. ErpICASSO allowed for separation of the novelty-related P3a and the top-down control-related P3b sub-components of P300. Specifically, the positive deflection identifiable as P3b, was significantly greater in the positive than in the negative priming group, while the late negative deflection corresponding to the parietal N400, was reduced in the positive priming group. The authors concluded that negative priming was related to specific processes at encoding which were inadequate such as attention and/or meaning retrieval, generating weak semantic representations and thus making words less accessible in subsequent implicit retrieval (Sebastiani et al., 2015).

Taken together, recent years have seen a rapid increase (especially among cognitive psychologists, cognitive neuroscientists, and developmental researchers) in the study of cross-modal correspondences—the tendency for our brains (not to mention the brains of other species) to preferentially associate certain features or dimensions of stimuli across the senses.

Empirical evidence has been provided supporting the existence of numerous cross-modal correspondences, affecting people's performance across a wide range of psychological tasks—in everything from the redundant target effect paradigm through to studies of the Implicit Association Test, and from speeded discrimination/classification tasks through to unspeeded spatial localization and temporal order judgment tasks.

However, one question that has yet to receive a satisfactory answer is whether cross-modal correspondences automatically affect people's performance (in all, or at least in a subset of tasks), as opposed to reflecting more of a strategic, or top-down, phenomenon. Here, in our discussion of the latest research on the topic of cross-modal correspondences, it appears that answering the question will require researchers to be more precise in terms of defining what exactly automaticity entails.

Furthermore, one's answer to the automaticity question may also hinge on the answer to a second question: Namely, whether cross-modal correspondences are all "of a kind," or whether instead there may be several different kinds of cross-modal mapping (e.g., statistical, structural, and semantic). Different answers to the automaticity question may then be revealed depending on the type of correspondence under consideration. Future research needs to determine just how automatic cross-modal correspondences really are (Spence & Deroy, 2013).

Chapter 6

Preserved and Impaired Priming Effects in Clinical Disorders

As previously stated, implicit memory is generally preserved in Alzheimer's disease (AD). However, some implicit priming effects are impaired and others are not. The preserved/impaired priming effects are often interpreted according to the perceptual/conceptual or identification/production distinctions.

Perceptual-identification priming paradigms are thought to be preserved and conceptual-production priming paradigms impaired. A third interpretation is yet possible based on the disconnection syndrome hypothesis which states that patients with AD should fail tasks requiring relatively complex brain communications. In this case, patients with AD should not demonstrate a significant perceptual priming effect in an identification task if it involves complex brain communications.

This latter hypothesis was evaluated with two cross-modal priming experiments using a categorization task. A visual meaningless mask was presented with half of the auditory primes in order to test the nature of the cross-modal priming effect. The control group exhibited significant priming effects for unmasked primes. The interference effect of the mask demonstrated that the priming effect was perceptually driven. Patients with AD did not exhibit any priming effect nor mask interference. These findings, therefore, showed that perceptual priming using an identification task was impaired in AD supporting the disconnection syndrome hypothesis (Vallet et al., 2013).

In order to investigate the basic mechanisms underlying normal repetition priming in AD, evoked by text re-reading procedures, reading facilitation elicited by previous reading or listening to a text was compared in a sample of AD patients (mean age 71.1 yrs.) and a group of age-matched normal controls. Consistent with previous evidence in normal undergraduates (Levy & Kirsner, 1989), previous listening to a text decreased the successive reading time of the same text (cross-modality priming). However, the reading facilitation elicited by previous reading of the same text (within modality priming) was significantly larger than the facilitation evoked by previous listening.

Compared to normal controls, AD patients showed intact cross modality and within modality priming. These data are discussed in the light of alternative hypotheses regarding the basic mechanisms of impaired and spared repetition priming in degenerative demented patients (Carlesimo, Mauri, Fadda, Turriziani, & Caltagirone, 2001). Hine and Tsushima (2018) found that implicit but not explicit memory was affected by the perception style of an individual. That is, individuals using a local perception style tended to use implicit memory to a greater extent than global perception style people.

Overall, preserved memory and evidence of prior learning in the absence of awareness can be demonstrated using a variety of techniques in various neurologic disorders but not in all disorders and only using select memory elicitation techniques.

Chapter 7

Language Learning, Artificial Grammars and Modality Effects

ARTIFICIAL GRAMMARS, RULE LEARNING AND IMPLICIT LEARNING

Many of the findings of both modality independence and modality specificity come from the field of statistical learning. Studies using the artificial grammar learning paradigm first designed by Reber (1967) have shown that participants can transfer their knowledge gained from one stimulus domain (e.g., visual symbols) to a different domain (e.g., nonsense syllables) if the underlying rule structure is the same (Silva, Folia, Inácio, Castro & Petersson, 2018). Generally, participants in artificial language studies display implicit knowledge of the sequential structure despite having minimal explicit awareness of the underlying rules of the language.

Frequently these studies report that most participants indicate they were guessing during the test task. A recent example is Silva and colleagues (2018), who demonstrated that this combination of implicit modality-specific knowledge with minimal explicit knowledge can be seen in structural, rule-based learning.

They argue that their results indicate differences in memory systems supporting structural learning may be key to explain modality-specific outcomes and support the idea of modality-specificity combined with modality-independence. They also argue that their results suggest that memory differences for visual vs. auditory sequences may contribute importantly to cross-modal differences (Silva, Folia, Inácio, Castro & Petersson, 2018).

Testing in the same modality as the learning context improves performance and different modalities yield differing amounts of learning, but what about implicit learning in more than one modality at a time? Conway and Pisoni

(2008) conducted a series of studies using two modalities at the same time and found that participants were just as good at the implicit learning of structural regularities from two different input streams as they were with only one, as long as the two input types were in different sense modalities or perceptual dimensions. The findings have been used to suggest that there could be parallel, independent implicit learning mechanisms for each specific type of perceptual input (Conway & Pisoni, 2008).

Broadly speaking, language is a rule-based system that allows for the creation of novel combinations of words in predictable ways. This system allows humans to communicate complex and novel ideas easily and efficiently making complex human functioning possible. Without a shared language, we would have to learn everything through experience and so it is hard to overstate the importance of language to human functioning. Language is also arguably the most complex system that humans have to learn primarily during the first few years of life. Other forms of complex learning like reading or algebra are not even attempted until much later in development. In contrast to most other cognitive skill levels which increase over the course of childhood, language-learning abilities decline after early childhood (Newport, 2020).

That is, children have particular skills in seemingly effortlessly capturing the complexities of their native language and second languages, with impressive speed and without explicit teaching. Although language learning is more difficult in older children and adults, humans retain the ability to learn new languages throughout the lifespan (Saffran, 2018). Language is a uniquely human ability and while other species have shown a capacity to communicate, some using complex sign language as an example, humans use language in ways that other animals do not (Burling et al., 1993).

So, what does all of this have to do with the inner world of unaware phenomena? The answer lies in the fact that the uniqueness of language combined with the effortless learning in the first few years of life make language one of the areas in which implicit learning has been studied extensively across a number of disciplinary areas and literatures. The biggest contributor to understanding language comes from research with young children. Infants are sensitive to the sounds made in every language at six months, but only the sounds made in languages they hear at 12 months, so the process of learning language starts very early and the perceptual narrowing in the first year of life facilitates learning of the languages spoken around a child (Breen, Pomper, & Saffran, 2019). Familiarity with the structure of the language we hear is helpful in segmenting the speech stream. For example, knowing that stressed syllables tend to initiate words in English allows a listener to correctly segment an utterance after a single hearing (Erickson & Thiessen, 2015).

Children learn language without explicit teaching across diverse contexts where they are exposed to language. In other words, the complex rules and structures underlying language are learned without explicit reference or awareness of the rule structures. In cultures where children are not spoken to directly, they still learn and in cases where they are not exposed to language they can use, they create one. Examples of this can be found in creole languages in which the children of displaced populations who speak multiple languages create a rule-based system from the pigeon combinations their parents use to communicate and deaf children have created their own form of sign language when there was no gestural language for them to learn (Goldin-Meadow, 2003).

To study language, researchers often use artificial language to see what and how people learn language. These artificial languages, also called mini languages, can be manipulated to be more or less predictive and have more or less consistent structure. Even within one of the artificial languages different phonemes can be more or less predictive of the next sound. This ability to manipulate the structure of the artificial language can be used to study the limits of sensitivity to regularities in the speech stream. Both infants and adults can use information about regularities in the speech stream to segment the stream of sound into phonemes and words (Levine, Buchsbaum, Hirsh-Pasek, Golinkoff, 2018; Newport, 2020).

Typically, subjects are exposed to letter strings generated by an artificial grammar and then shown new letter strings to classify as grammatical or not. With adults this is done either visually or aurally. With infants, the artificial grammar is presented aurally and a habituation paradigm allows researchers to see if the infants are surprised by non-grammatical sequences at test.

Studies using these artificial languages find that infants and young children as well as adults use the statistical information from the distribution of different elements in speech to determine things like what sequences of sound form the morphemes and words of the language (Reeder, Newport, & Aslin, 2013; Saffran, Aslin & Newport, 1996). Children form implicit rules from language input that are applied in a fairly deterministic way. Surprisingly, they show the same rule-like and deterministic behavior even when the relevant grammatical forms in the language input are used inconsistently.

Adults, on the other hand, match the frequency of the input. When a form is used inconsistently or probabilistically, without a conditioning context, adult learners reproduce the statistical inconsistencies or probabilities of that form in the input. This probability matching behavior is not characteristic of young child learners, either in naturalistic data or in laboratory experiments (Newport, 2019).

Another important factor is knowledge about which syllables are usually stressed in a language. For example, stressed syllables in English allow a listener to correctly segment an utterance after a single hearing. English-speaking infants and adults are more accurate at segmenting a speech stream with the stress pattern typical to English speech (e.g., Thiessen & Erickson, 2013a; Thiessen & Saffran, 2003).

As alluded to earlier, Conway and Pisoni's (2008) review found indications that there is an implicit system to handle learning of word-like sounds that appears to be closely involved in language learning and processing. They found that participants were as good at learning structural regularities from two input streams as from one, as long as the two streams were in different sensory modalities or perceptual dimensions. That lack of interference from other implicit tasks implies that the implicit system that is sensitive to the regularities that allow us to learn language are specific to learning structures that can be represented as phonological information.

Manifestations of language impairments in different clinical populations might be produced by distinct patterns of disruptions to the machinery responsible for sensitivity to structure (Erickson & Thiessen, 2015). Specific language impairments can be independent of other developmental impairments and be comorbid with other developmental disorders (e.g., autism). Language impairments can exhibit great heterogeneity both with respect to manifestation and severity. This likely results from the fact that specific language impairment is diagnosed when a child's oral language lags behind other areas of development for reasons that cannot be ascertained. Studies indicate that sensitivity to conditional structure is impaired in specific language impairment which may be related to both the small vocabularies found in specific language impaired individuals and difficulties acquiring linguistic patterns (Erickson & Thiessen, 2015).

Language learning has also been studied in amnesia patients. Using an artificial grammar, Knowlton, Ramus and Squire (1992) exposed participants to their novel grammar and asked amnesia patents and controls to classify new letter strings as grammatical or non-grammatical. Amnesic patients performed similarly to healthy controls. However, compared with controls, amnesic patients struggled on a recognition test of the exemplars that had been presented. Amnesic patients also struggled compared to controls when instructed to classify new letter strings when compared with the original exemplars.

These results suggest that classification learning based an artificial grammar can be normal even when participants have impaired memory for the exemplars themselves (Knowlton, Ramus & Squire, 1992). In other words, despite being unaware of the underlying rules, the artificial grammar could still be learned despite the fact that memory for the exemplars was impaired.

As previously alluded to language learning in the real world is a uniquely human ability that makes most of our complex social structures possible. Language is also unique in how quickly and easily human infants learn the languages spoken around them. The robustness of the implicit processes mediating language learning is supported by the fact that even individuals with neurodevelopmental challenges can still master the core grammar underlying their first language. Issues with early language learning and expression are often the first sign of a number of developmental delays and disabilities and language is also a sensitive measure for indicating the location and severity of damage from a stroke or traumatic brain injury.

Chapter 8

Statistical Learning
and Pattern Detection

Streams of events are part of our daily existence and people are generally very good at figuring out where and when these events begin and end. Adults easily recognize boundaries in continuous streams of activity and information that usually indicate things to which they should be attending. Segmenting events is necessary for proficient functioning in the world. In order to effectively operate in the world, individuals need to understand what other people are doing and what is happening in the world around them (Levine, Buchsbaum, Hirsh-Pasek, & Golinkoff, 2018).

This ability to detect regularities in the world and use them to function is called statistical learning in much of the recent literature. The term statistical learning has been somewhat controversial in the research. Although it was used before this, the seminal work of Saffran and colleagues has been the recent standard by which statistical learning is measured (1996 paper and a few others).

In the first of these papers, Saffran and colleagues found that infants at eight months of age could use frequency of sound pairings to segment speech streams into morphemes and words. Following that, further studies showed that adults and older children could also use frequencies to parse language. Interestingly, this research fostered a large number of studies into the ability of people to detect and respond to regularities in their environment that are below the level of conscious awareness. The difficulties with this area of research have to do with a lack of specificity in the definition of statistical learning.

There are broader definitions like the ability to find patterns in the input provided (Romberg & Saffran, 2010) that do not address the question of implicit learning or unawareness. Definitions such as "adaptation to the regularities of the world that evolves without intention to learn, and without clear awareness of what we know" (Perruchet & Pacton, 2006, p. 233) acknowledge the role of implicit learning and unawareness in statistical learning.

CHILDREN AND STATISTICAL LEARNING

The process of extracting subtle patterns in the environment happens throughout the lifespan. This type of learning was first reported in 8-month-old infants, who were briefly exposed to a continuous stream of repeating three-syllable nonsense words. Following exposure, infants showed sensitivity to the difference between the three-syllable sequences and foil sequences made up of the same syllables recombined in a different order, demonstrating that they were able to use the statistics of the input stream to discover word boundaries in connected speech (Saffran, Aslin, & Newport, 1996).

This finding had a huge impact on research into language acquisition. It showed that humans can use a general sensitivity to statistical information to help acquire language. Statistical learning has been found in older children and adults as well as infants (e.g., Fiser & Aslin, 2001, 2002). This kind of learning allows learners to detect regularities in the environment and use those regularities to segment the world into meaningful units. There is also evidence that this ability is available quite early and emerges as a consequence of experience.

There is also evidence of automaticity. That is, participants often report they are guessing or they don't know and yet in a forced choice situation they are successful far beyond chance. In other words, regularities are detected and processed via mechanisms beyond conscious awareness. Statistical learning is most often used in studies examining artificial grammar learning but other types of implicit learning seem to show similar pattern detection. Some recent results provide evidence that explicit learning is co-occurring during statistical learning and that the explicit learning component may be dissociable from the implicit learning component (Batterink, Reber, Neville & Paller, 2015).

In experiments with adults, participants are exposed to a stream of repeating three-syllable nonsense words, much like in the original infant study by Saffran and colleagues. Learning is usually assessed using a forced-choice recognition test. On each trial, participants are presented with a pair of stimuli: a nonsense word from the exposure stream and another composed of syllables from the speech stream combined in a novel order. They are asked which stimulus sounds more familiar, the word based on the initial familiarization stream or the one using syllables from the initial stream out of order. Statistical learning can be said to have occurred if participants choose the word that fits the familiarization pattern on the recognition test more often than would be predicted by chance.

Statistical learning can and often does happen without instruction or any conscious attempts to find the pattern. When stimuli are presented passively without any explicit task or when participants are engaged in an unrelated cover task, they are still sensitive to the statistical regularities in the stimuli. In addition, participants in statistical learning studies seem to have little explicit knowledge of the underlying statistical structure of the stimuli when assessed during debriefing (e.g., Conway & Christiansen, 2005).

Developmental Characteristics of Statistical Learning

Newport (2019) argues that the findings in infants and adults show statistical biases in learning that change as a function of age over the participants' lifespan. These biases are an important part of the processes that shape languages of the world. That is, research suggests that young children appear to be biased toward forming categorical rules while older children and adults appear to be more able to acquire probabilistic variations. Newport argues that further research using artificial miniature languages will help to provide insights into the processes and the developmental changes that occur in natural language acquisition (Newport, 2019).

Amnestic patients show intact performance on several statistical learning tasks even though they have greatly reduced or nonexistent explicit memory (Knowlton, Ramus, & Squire, 1992; Knowlton & Squire, 1994, 1996). These findings support the claim that explicit knowledge of the training materials or underlying sequence is not necessary for statistical learning to occur on these tasks.

The linkage to the world of unaware phenomenon is that these findings indicate that item-specific knowledge including but not limited to memory of specific letter strings can be acquired without declarative memory. Moreover, implicit knowledge can also support classification performance without explicit awareness (Knowlton & Squire, 1996).

In the real world, statistical learning allows us to pick out the regularities that shape the edges of events so we know when to attend to boundary information, such as the beginning and end of an event, a word, a sentence, a pattern in any modality. This information makes the world more predictable and reduces the cognitive load of processing familiar events.

Chapter 9

Neurologic and Neuropsychiatric Perspectives

PROSOPAGNOSIA AND EVIDENCE FOR COVERT RECOGNITION

The world of unaware phenomena can also extend to prosopagnosia. Prosopagnosic patients have an inability to recognize faces that ought to be familiar. Although familiar faces may evoke no sense or feeling of familiarity, prosopagnosic patients are capable of recognizing familiar people in other ways. For example, they can recognize people by their voice, gait, or clothing (Diamond, Mayes & Meudell, 1995). In addition, they can provide accurate and appropriate semantic information about familiar people on hearing or seeing their name as well as match photographs of unfamiliar faces (Young & De Haan, 1992).

From a neuroanatomic perspective, prosopagnosia is believed to be produced by bilateral damage in the occipitotemporal cortices, or in their forward projections. In a majority of patients (although there are exceptions), following post-mortem examination, damage is generally represented bilaterally (Damasio, 1985; Meadows, 1974). However, there is evidence suggesting that a right hemisphere lesion alone may be sufficient to produce prosopagnosia (Diamond, Mayes & Meudell, 1994; Landis et al., 1988 De Renzi, 1986).

With respect to underlying mechanisms, it has been posited that in prosopagnosia the perceptual encoding of faces that ought to be familiar fail to evoke memories associated with those faces. And whatever memories are evoked may be weakly represented. Several varieties of prosopagnosia appear to exist, one involving a perceptual deficit and the other involving a disconnection of normal perceptual processes from memory (see De Renzi et al., 1991, and McNeil & Warrington, 1991).

A number of frameworks and models have been proposed in order to explain prosopagnosia. The framework proposed by Bruce and Young (1986) is generally consistent with the patterns of breakdown seen in the literature. The model provides an outline for multiple stages putatively involved in recognizing a familiar face. The first stage involves forming a structural description of a face. Representations of familiar faces are stored in what are called face recognition units (FRUs). It is proposed that there is one FRU for each known face. So, you would have an FRU for your mother and for your father and for your best friend. If the structural description of a stimulus face matches the representation of a known face, the appropriate FRU becomes activated.

Following activation, retrieval of semantic information associated with the face would take place. The semantic information is not conceptualized as part of the FRU system, but is instead accessed via a functionally distinct and separate "person identity node" (PIN). In the final stage of the process, the appropriate name code for the recognized person is retrieved. The name code retrieval process is viewed as separate from semantic information retrieval and can only be accessed via the person identity node.

A variety of measures and techniques have been used to show evidence of covert recognition including physiological and behavioral measures. For example, discriminating correct from incorrect famous and familiar face-name matches has been achieved using electrodermal measures (Bauer, 1984, 1986) including discriminating familiar versus unfamiliar faces (Tranel & Damasio, 1985, 1988). Behavioral evidence of implicit memory has been demonstrated in tasks showing patterns of semantic facilitation, and interference in learning and priming tasks (Bruyer et al., 1983; De Haan, Young & Newcombe, 1987; Young & De Haan, 1988) produced by familiar, but unrecognized faces,

Sergent and Poncet (1990) found that patient PV, despite an inability to recognize familiar people from their faces, could nevertheless demonstrate memory for these faces in tasks that did not require explicit recognition. So, for example, PV showed enhanced learning of correct famous face-name matches versus incorrect matches (replicated by Diamond, Mayes & Meudel, 1994). These authors also reported cued-recognition in a task which required a selection of the name corresponding to the presented famous face. However, the cued recognition remained covert, without the patient experiencing any conscious sense of familiarity. This effect has been replicated by De Haan et al. (1991) and McNeil and Warrington (1991).

However, it should be noted that covert recognition of faces in prosopagnosics has not been always been found. Bauer (1986) reported that familiar correct face-name matches failed to elicit electrodermal responses in patient GY. In order to explain this finding, it was suggested that GY was impaired in the perceptual analysis and synthesis of incoming information, which interfered with the process of activating stored internal representations of the face irrespective of whether processing was driven by aware or unaware processes. Newcombe et al. (1989), Sergent and Villemure (1989) and Young and Ellis (1989) found that the tasks that had previously elicited semantic facilitation in priming and learning in prosopagnosics failed to do so in their patients.

In order to better understand the complexities underlying face processing in prosopagnosia, Burton et al. (1991) used the IAC network to simulate covert recognition in prosopagnosia by suggesting that the impairment is a weakening of the links between FRUs and PINs. They proposed that the FRUs are intact and pass some activation to the PINs. However, the activation from FRUs is not sufficient to raise the activation of the PIN above the threshold required for overt recognition.

Thus, below threshold or residual activation is sufficient to account for semantic priming and interference effects from unrecognized famous faces, but is not sufficient for eliciting conscious and aware memory. Burton et al. suggest the pattern of deficits in a prosopagnosic patient who did not show covert recognition (MS) can be simulated in a variety of ways, but the critical point is that no activation reached the PINs. It should be emphasized that the Burton et al. (1991) model of prosopagnosia leads to an interesting prediction. That is, a prosopagnosic patient who shows covert recognition should be able to make the correct forced choice of the name of a depicted known, but unrecognized face.

Because PINs receive activation from names, when a person sees or hears a familiar name, the activation of the PIN would increase for that individual thus pushing it above threshold. Once activation is supra-threshold, the patient should be able to respond to the correct face-name match, because the relevant PIN will also be receiving residual activation from the face. This difference in activation over PINs corresponding to other presented names should be detectable, as the activation is boosted to supra-threshold levels. This prediction has been confirmed by the prosopagnosic patient reported by Sergent and Poncet (1990).

The ability to make correct face-name matches has also been reported in several studies with amnesic patients for whom familiar faces evoke a feeling of familiarity, but who could not access semantic information (De Haan, Young & Newcombe, 1991; McNeil & Warrington, 1991). Although this latter result is predicted by the IAC model, it is less striking as the patient obtains a sense of familiarity from both known faces and names.

A case-study of a patient (ET) who suffered from prosopagnosia following a traumatic brain injury, who despite severe perceptual difficulties in tests involving non-face stimuli and in matching unfamiliar faces, nevertheless showed evidence of "covert" recognition of faces that should have been

familiar (Diamond, Mayes & Meudel, 1994). While ET was densely prosopagnosic, she nevertheless performed at normal levels in word and object
recognition tasks and was unimpaired in her ability to recognize names of
celebrities. She performed at the same level as controls in her ability to make
a forced-choice of the correct name for a famous face, even though the face
evoked no feeling of familiarity for her. Performance was at only chance
levels in a forced-choice face familiarity decision task, but importantly, she
showed evidence of covert recognition in a "true" versus "untrue" face-name
learning task.

In other words, while performing at only chance levels on a face familiarity
task, she did exhibit enhanced learning on true versus untrue face-name pairings. So, for example, she would more effectively learn the pairing of Albert
Einstein's face with his name thus showing evidence that prior learning facilitated "new" learning. In this instance, the world of unaware knowledge was
accessed via an indirect route. That is, facilitation of learning without explicit
reference to prior knowledge and associations (Diamond, Mayes & Meudell,
1994). In addition, ET correctly matched 19 out of 22 faces and names (correct proportion = .86, z = -.57) which was not significantly different from the
controls' level of performance of 20 out of 22 (proportion correct = .90, SD =
.07). Thus, despite the fact that ET expressed no sense of familiarity for any
of the faces, she correctly matched faces with correct names on 86 percent
of the trials, always feeling as if she was merely guessing but she clearly
exceeded chance.

ET also showed conscious and aware recognition of some famous faces by
using a procedure based on Sergent and Poncet's (1990) semantic activation
task. Basically, famous faces were grouped according to semantic category
(i.e., singers, actors) and the activation induced by exposure to multiple faces
drawn from the same semantic category appears to have induced conscious
recognition by exceeding an activation threshold.

The pattern of ET's face processing impairments was interpreted in terms
of an interactive activation model of face processing. Of relevance to this text
is the fact that access to information and associations appears to have been
beyond the reach of conscious, willful retrieval and awareness. However, the
associations were accessible via less direct pathways that were expressed in
a variety of ways, that is, through enhanced learning and weak internal feedback that influenced her behavior in ways beyond her conscious awareness.
In contrast to the unaware expression of prior learning, the semantic activation procedure did, in fact, induce aware face recognition, thus providing a
potential pathway for inaccessible and unaware phenomena . . . into aware
and conscious manifestations.

ANXIETY

The world of unaware phenomena may play a role in our understanding of how automatic biases are expressed in individuals with various psychological disorders, in terms of how they view themselves, the social world, and in their vulnerability to psychopathology especially in anxiety disorders (Teachman, Cody, & Clerkin, 2010). Specifically, cognitive theories of depression have expressed the idea that individuals with depression carry with them self-referential representations (i.e., themes of loss, failure, worthlessness, rejection and hopelessness) that can be activated by environmental triggers. Triggers can be negative memories or emotions that activate other nodes in a complex associative network.

These self-schemas can generate automatic and systematic biases that influence information processing in ways beyond the awareness of the individual (Phillips, Hine, & Thorsteinsson, 2010). Additional support for the idea of latent depressogenic self-schemas comes from the work of de Raedt who posited that an inability to disengage from these schemas leads to vulnerability for depression. Teachman and Woody (2004) examined automatic processes in anxiety and the maladaptive fear schemata that alter the allocation of attentional resources toward stimuli perceived as threatening.

It is proposed that these attentional biases result from schemata that misclassify innocuous stimuli as dangerous and ambiguous stimuli as threatening (Segal, 1996), with many of these processes occurring on an implicit and unaware level. In essence, an individual's cognitive framework creates a lens through which the world is perceived as dangerous and where automatic thoughts and associations influence higher-level cognitive processes, contributing to subjective anxiety.

Addictive Behavior

Bowler, Bowler, and James (2011) evaluated the role of implicit biases in addictive behavior, concluding that addiction-prone individuals are influenced by cognitive biases that rationalize self-destructive behavior and that these processes predict or correlate with addictive behaviors. There is additional research suggesting that implicit cognitive processing theory can play an important role in alcohol research as there is evidence indicating that implicit cognition reliably predicts substance use (Rooke, Hine, & Thorsteinsson, 2008).

Similarly, Wiers et al. (2002) showed that implicit memories of alcohol associations are significant predictors of alcohol use and that implicit retrieval processes influence alcohol outcome expectancies and consumption.

Moreover, alcohol consumption impacts implicit memory processing and can also alter attentional bias and implicit associations. Changes in implicit alcohol cognitions may help mediate alcohol-induced priming of the incentive to drink (Field, Wiers, Christiansen, Fillmore & Verster, 2010).

Thus, implicit cognitions and memories can alter our use and abuse of various substances including alcohol and may provide a potential therapeutic tool with which to treat these disorders. By identifying and altering implicit cognitions, clinicians may be able to disrupt networks of dysfunctional and unaware associations that help foster substance use disorders.

Clearly, the world of unaware phenomena can impact our health and well-being in ways that are not immediately obvious but nevertheless alter how we react to the world, feel about ourselves and cope with life's stressors.

Anosognosia

Brain injury is often accompanied by a variety of deficits affecting multiple cognitive, motor, perceptual and affective domains. However, a significant number of individuals with brain injury also exhibit unawareness of the fact that they have severely debilitating deficits affecting the domains of language, motor and memory function among others (McGlynn, & Schacter, 1989).

Anosognosia, at its most fundamental level, is characterized by a denial or unawareness of deficit or illness where a patient may explicitly deny an illness and/or may exhibit what appears to be apathy regarding the deficit. Explicit denial has been termed anosognosia and anosodiaphoria refers to indifference (Critchley, 1953). Anosognosia has been characterized as multi-factorial and expressed across diverse clinical manifestations that vary from patient to patient (Cocchini, Beschin, Della Sala (2012).

In Wernicke's aphasia, patients have fluent speech with neologisms and phonemic and semantic paraphasic errors. Patients often exhibit impairments in comprehension, naming, repetition, reading and writing. Wernicke's aphasia patients, because of functional deficits, do not manifest a verbally mediated explicit denial of illness. However, they make no attempt at correcting phonemic errors and they characteristically will be angered or frustrated when they are not understood, despite the incomprehensibility of their speech (Alajouanine, 1956). This pattern of behavior suggests that they have an unawareness of deficit.

It appears that while similar and common mechanisms may underlie anosognosia across a diverse spectrum of deficits, it is associated with multiple specific deficits. Thus, memory impairments interfere with the ability to remember memory failures, resulting in a diminished awareness of the nature and severity of memory performance (Hannesdottir & Morris, 2007). It has been proposed that lack of verbal comprehension accounts for the anosognosia associated with aphasia (Lebrun, 1987). In neglect syndromes, patients may neglect or ignore half of the food on a dinner plate or, in the winter, place gloves on only one hand. In fact, there are patients who show no awareness that they have a paralysis on one side of their body and it has been suggested that neglect syndrome may account for unawareness of hemiplegia (Cocchini et al., 2002).

Blindsight

Blindsight is a clinically verified visual field defect due to destruction or dysfunction to primary visual cortex (V1) resulting in chronic blindness. However, some patients who lack visual awareness may, nevertheless, exhibit visually guided behavior, a phenomenon which has been labeled blindsight (Leopold, 2012). Blindsight represents yet another manifestation of an unaware phenomenon whereby individuals exhibit an ability to detect, localize and discriminate visual stimuli. There is an important and fascinating caveat as an individual may deny seeing anything (Cowey, 2010).

Blindsight may provide insight into the mechanisms mediating visual processing when there is damage or dysfunction in the primary visual cortex but it also provides another example of implicit knowledge and it has, over the years, attracted the attention of neuropsychologists, neuroscientists and an occasional philosopher.

In a series of experiments examining blindsight, it was concluded that aspects of shape are much better perceived in blindsight than previously thought and it was theorized that the main deficit in blindsight is one of consciousness. Evidence supporting this notion is based on findings suggesting that subjects have been consistently semantically biased to a significant degree by words in the blind field and that indirect methods, for example priming, are more sensitive to revealing non-conscious perception than direct ones such as forced-choice protocols. Moreover, the experiments also indicated that orientation, curvature, structural descriptions and spatial ordering of letters are processed non-consciously in the blind field as well (Marcel, 1998).

In fact, there are multiple reports of patients responding to stimuli such as shapes, faces, semantic information, moving and flashing stimuli presented within visual field regions that are characterized as phenomenally blind (Fendrich, Wessinger & Gazzaniga, 2001). Furthermore, blindsight has also been reported in monkeys with research exploring the effects of removing parts or all of V1 in monkeys and evaluating residual cerebral capabilities to respond to visual stimuli in their defective visual fields (Cowey, 2010).

With respect to underlying mechanisms, it has been argued that blindsight may depend on vestiges of geniculostriate function. In order to account for the frequency of blindsight within residual islands of function, there is speculation that patients may be unaware of such islands because they are, in fact, *islands* and are, therefore, isolated from the fully integrated neural network that represents a person's visual space (Fendrich, Wessinger & Gazzaniga, 2001).

While evidence gleaned from imaging techniques has suggested to some that V1 may mediate conscious perception (Leopold, 2012), others have posited that blindsight may have its roots in the phylogenetic origins of our visual pathways. That is, both the phenomena of neglect and hemianopia may have their origins in what has been referred to as a disrupted dynamic interplay between cortical visual pathways and more phylogenetically primitive visual pathways linked to the midbrain (Ro & Rafal, 2006). In fact, blindsight is a type of hemianopia and there is speculation that blindsight may be mediated by subcortical processes and/or compensatory use of spared visual function.

These putative mechanisms may have implications with respect to the rehabilitation of visual processing deficits. In other words, these mechanisms appear to support visual information processing in the absence of conscious awareness, perhaps providing a route and modality to rehabilitate patients with damage to areas affecting cortically mediated visual processing.

It should be noted that blindsight is a phenomenon that remains controversial. For example, is "blindsight" truly blind? There are reports that some individuals report vague experiences when reporting correctly about stimuli (Overgaard, 2012), whereas other individuals have reported no experiences. According to Overgaard (2011), in order to accommodate the diverse findings that have been reported in the literature, a viable interpretation may be that blindsight is associated with some level of preserved visual function that exists co-temporaneously with severely degraded visual processing and expression. It has also been speculated that there may be sub-varieties of blindsight or that it may vary on a continuum of severity.

While V1 does appear to play a vital role in primate vision, Leopold (2012) found little evidence supporting a role in mediating visual awareness. What we do know is that striate cortical lesions are capable of producing dissociations between visual performance and visual awareness. Moreover, there is evidence that blindsight is not an example of normal, near-threshold vision. That is, in blindsight, stimuli appear to be processed in what has been characterized as an unusual manner (Azzopardi & Cowey, 1997).

But what we do know is that you can throw a ball to some with blindsight, and they will catch it, although they may deny that there was any ball present. In other words, they could track and accommodate to the ball's trajectory but are unaware of the ball or at least the feedback they are receiving does not appear to be sufficient to induce conscious awareness.

PTSD and Unawareness

It has been estimated that exposure to traumatic events may affect the lives of 50–70% of the general population (Kessler et al., 1995). Posttraumatic stress disorder (PTSD) is a disorder that develops in a subset of individuals who have experienced scary, shocking or dangerous events or perhaps lost a loved one. It can also develop in individuals who have not experienced the trauma directly but experience such events vicariously.

PTSD can develop across the lifespan and can include a wide variety of individuals, backgrounds and situations including war veterans, children, and people who have experienced physical or sexual assault, accidents, abuse, or natural or man-made disasters. Individuals so affected can experience flash-backs, problems falling or staying asleep, anger, fear and avoidance of stimuli that evoke memories of the trauma (American Psychiatric Association, 2013).

Moreover, epidemiological studies suggest that women are at greater risk for developing PTSD (Olff, Langeland, Draijer, & Gersons, 2007; Tolin & Foa, 2006). While most people recover from stressful and traumatic events within 6 months, some individuals experience delayed onset of symptoms, months later, and in some instances, symptoms may emerge many years after the initial exposure to trauma and thus the condition can become chronic (Gold et al., 2000). Symptoms must last for more than a month and be severe enough to interfere with social relationships or work in order to be diagnosed with PTSD (DSM-V, 2013).

There are some recent findings suggesting that disruptions of sleep-related memory processing may mediate the development of posttraumatic stress symptoms. However, there are discrepant findings with some work suggest-ing that if exposure to a traumatic event is followed by sleep this results in fewer intrusive memories, while other work suggests just the opposite. That is, fewer intrusive memories will be associated with sleep deprivation (Sopp, Brueckner, Schäfer, Lass-Hennemann & Michael, 2019).

Sopp et al. (2019) report finding higher explicit memory for potential trauma reminders after sleep as compared to partial sleep deprivation. Interestingly, no group differences were found for implicit memory. In other words, implicit, unaware memory versus explicit memory did not appear to be sensitive to manipulations of sleep.

One might ask what this has to do with the inner world of unaware phe-nomena. Simply put, the linkages are gradually emerging. However, there are findings suggesting that in veterans with PTSD, patients demonstrate an implicit memory bias for combat-relevant sentences, whereas controls do not. This finding may suggest a differential priming effect whereby threat-related information is automatically accessed in individuals diagnosed with PTSD (Amir, McNally & Wiegartz, 1996).

In other words, the threshold for accessing trauma-related memories is lower and access can occur in the absence of conscious, willful retrieval, essentially automatically. Adverse reactions to stress-related events may be elicited by words, images, sounds, or scents and expressed in ways that influence behavior and physiology but in the absence of any awareness of the linkages between prior events and the eliciting stimuli.

There is research showing that exposure to extremely stressful events affects brain function and that traumatized individuals may be vulnerable to exaggerated reactions to sensory information. The greater incidence of PTSD in women may be mediated via hyperactivation of fear-processing networks (Olff et al., 2007). If the threshold for activating these networks in women following trauma is lower, this may result in a sustained state of arousal which may then elevate risk for developing PTSD (Bryant, Creamer, O'Donnell, Silove, & McFarlane, 2008).

Reactions to stress may be subcortically mediated and result in responses that are disproportionate and not relevant to current conditions and contexts and may, in fact, be harmful. Stimuli or cues related to trauma can automatically and without conscious awareness or mediation activate brain regions that support intense emotions, and result in decreased activation in the central nervous system (CNS) regions involved in the integration of sensory input with motor output; the modulation of physiological arousal, and the capacity to communicate experience in words.

Individuals diagnosed with PTSD may experience failures of attention and memory that interfere with their capacity to engage in the present. In essence, traumatized individuals "lose their way in the world" and some research suggests that effective treatment needs to involve (1) learning to tolerate feelings and sensations by increasing the capacity for interception, (2) learning to modulate arousal, and (3) learning that after confrontation with physical helplessness it is essential to engage in taking effective action (Van Der Kolk, 2006).

Body-oriented therapies that emphasize guiding the client's attention to interoceptive, kinesthetic, and proprioceptive experience (i.e., Somatic Experiencing® [SE]) can be used to directly confront clinical issues in PTSD and lead to the resolution or mitigation of symptoms resulting from chronic and traumatic stress (Payne, Levine, Crane-Godreau, 2015).

The inner world of unaware phenomena plays a role in the lives of individuals who are traumatized as these individuals may be totally unaware of interoceptive processes that can affect the ways in which physical sensations and emotions rooted in the past influence attitudes and reaction patterns to events in the present.

This approach is based on the premise that one's past experiences are manifested and expressed in current psychophysiological states and action tendencies and that the trauma and stressful events are reenacted and expressed in breathing, gestures, sensory perceptions, movement, and emotion. All of which may be beyond the conscious awareness of the individual. In fact, in order for the therapeutic approach to be effective, the patient, rather than exclusively concentrating on the *meaning* of their experience, should also focus on physical self-experience and increase their level of self-awareness, thus piercing through the veil of unawareness that shrouds much of our everyday existence.

By reaching into the inner world of unaware phenomena and facilitating greater self-awareness, self-regulation and self-experience, therapeutic effectiveness may be enhanced. This self-awareness will be associated with and foster a greater awareness of one's sensations and action tendencies, which can facilitate self-discovery. This self-discovery can lead to new ways of orienting oneself to one's surroundings and explore novel ways of fostering potential sources of mastery and pleasure (Van Der Kolk, 2006). Interpersonal trauma often results in a fear of intimacy that in many traumatized individuals, automatically evokes implicit memories of being hurt, betrayed, and abandoned.

This fear of intimacy and the reality of making oneself seen, if not understood, can activate processes that re-invoke and cause the reliving of past victimization. Therapeutic techniques that help individuals learn how to develop a physical sense of control and an ability to regulate physiological arousal and retrieve and re-invoke prior experiences of safety and memories that affirm a sense of pleasure, empowerment and enjoyment can be effective treatment techniques. Pivotal to the process is a heightened sense of self, identification of the triggers and reactions, all of which can lead to greater self-awareness.

Chapter 10

Illuminating the Unaware World of Confabulation

AWARENESS AND CONFABULATION: ILLUMINATING THE UNAWARE WORLD

Ruptured and repaired aneurysms of the anterior communicating artery (ACoA) may result in a wide range of neurocognitive impairments including profound impairments in memory and executive function with some patients exhibiting confabulation (Diamond et al. 1996; DeLuca & Diamond, 1995). Moscovitch (1989) proposed that confabulation represents an inability to monitor the accuracy (or appropriateness) of a response.

DeLuca and Cicerone (1991) proposed a "dual-lesion" hypothesis of confabulation that invoked the idea of combined frontal and basal forebrain involvement. Relatedly, Johnson (1991) proposed that the unawareness associated with confabulation results from damage to a system(s) mediating the retrieval and validation of relevant memories and that theories of "unawareness" are likely mediated by frontal and perhaps basal forebrain system damage—the same areas that are thought to produce confabulation (Damasio, 1995). Achieving a better understanding of confabulation may provide insight into the nature and mechanisms underlying awareness.

There are two primary types of confabulation: spontaneous and provoked confabulation. (Kopelman, 1987). Provoked confabulation has been characterized as a "normal" response to a demand for information but because of some type of underlying pathology information remains inaccessible to conscious awareness. These confabulations often involve episodic memory, or memories for a person's autobiographic events that are retrieved out of their accurate chronological order (Dalla Barba, Boissé, Bartolomeo & Bachoud-Lévi, 1997).

For example, a patient who had been hospitalized, when asked how she spent the previous night, responds by saying that she went out to dinner in a nearby town with her husband. The problem is her husband has been deceased for 10 years and she spent the previous week in the hospital. However, this scenario is not implausible, as the patient had often gone to dinner in this nearby town with her husband, but the event was no longer linked to its accurate temporal context. She was asked a question and searched for information that was relevant and linked to well-established neural arrays. However, the information that was retrieved while accurate in its substance was uncoupled from its temporal context and thus she was unaware that the activity she described had occurred over 10 years earlier.

In contrast to provoked confabulation, spontaneous confabulation may involve implausible, bizarre or fantastic scenarios that are evoked during the course of informal everyday conversations. These confabulations may not necessarily be elicited by direct questioning (Dalla Barba et al., 1997) and they are characteristically both endorsed and acted upon by the patient (Schnider, 1999).

Confabulations are also "statements or actions that involve unintentional but obvious distortions" (Moscovitch & Mello, 1997). However, it should be emphasized that confabulations are not willful, conscious distortions of reality, but they appear instead, to be the product of a reconstructive process (DeLuca, 2001; Moscovitch, 1995) during the course of trying to remember. The evoked re-constructions appear to be largely beyond the confabulator's awareness and self-monitoring.

There are theories that attempt to explain confabulation and they generally fall into three major categories: the memory impairment model (Talland, Sweet & Ballantine, 1967); the executive impairment model (Kapur & Coughlan, 1980; Johnson, Hashroudi, & Lindsay, 1993; Benson et al., 1996) and the dual memory-dysexecutive model that suggests memory or executive dysfunction alone cannot explain confabulation (DeLuca & Diamond, 1995; DeLuca, 2000).

There are variants of these models including the "Temporal" theory (Talland, 1965) that suggests a disruption in the processes mediating temporal order judgments (Kopelman, 1989; Milner, Petrides, & Smith, 1985; Shimamura, Janowsky & Squire, 1991; Vriezen & Moscovitch, 1990); source amnesia for events over a lifetime (Schacter, 1987; Shimamura & Squire, 1987); the "retrieval" theory which states that confabulation is a primary deficit in retrieval (Lhermitte & Signoret, 1976) and there are also variants of the retrieval theory that sub-divide retrieval into strategic (i.e., effortful and directed) and associative (i.e., automatic or cue-driven [Moskovitch, 1989, 1995; Moscovitch, 1995]).

What mechanisms underlie confabulation? Retrieval theorists propose that confabulation is due to impairments in an individual's ability to monitor output and inhibit responses (Stuss et al., 1986; Shapiro, Alexander, Gardner & Mercer, 1981). Johnson (1991) and Johnson, Hashtroudi and Lindsay (1993) have proposed a "reality monitoring" framework whereby memories for external information (i.e., perceived or actual events) are distinguished from internally generated information (i.e., memories for thoughts or imaginations) by virtue of the fact that real event memories exhibit more salient perceptual characteristics (e.g., color, sound, smell), contextual information (e.g., spatial and temporal location), and affective as well as semantic information (Johnson et al., 1993).

Therefore, based on this framework, it is posited that differentiating external realty from internally generated information is contingent on the saliency, context and affective characteristics of the information. This may give rise to an interesting dilemma. That is, patients who are confabulating are likely unaware of whether information is internally or externally generated. Moreover, perceptual similarity between internal memories versus external sources can induce confusion and ambiguity between these two types of memories as well (Johnson, Foley, & Leach, 1988; Johnson, Raye, Wang, & Taylor, 1979).

Taken together, confabulation appears to be a disorder of awareness, information retrieval, and executive dysfunction that impact self-monitoring, awareness of temporal context, substantive accuracy and source (i.e., internal versus external). Can we find a way to distinguish confabulations from realities in an individual for whom the real and the unreal is beyond their conscious awareness? The short answer is, perhaps, using physiological measures.

A case study was conducted involving WP, a 61-year-old right-handed male, who suffered an aneurysm affecting the anterior communicating artery (ACoA) and who suffered a subsequent subarachnoid hemorrhage (Diamond, DeLuca, & Richards, 2003). A brain computed tomography (CT) scan showed infarcts affecting the basal forebrain region, right basal ganglia and inferior frontoparietal regions. At the time of testing, WP was 10 weeks post-stroke and was a florid confabulator.

He was given a computer-based "Confabulation, Autobiographical and Retrograde Scale (C-CAR)" which was a visually presented multiple-choice test consisting of eleven questions based on WP's autobiographical and confabulatory responses from prior weeks. Seven questions were based on confabulations that WP provided during his first testing session. The four remaining questions tapped information that WP had answered correctly during a previous session. The program displayed each question for five seconds, followed by three response options consisting of two incorrect and one correct option.

WP was instructed to "silently think about each option." After the third option was cleared from the screen, all three options were presented on the screen for five seconds. WP was asked to "choose one and only one option." Upon completion of each trial, WP was asked to rate his confidence for each answer based on a 5-point Likert scale (i.e., 1= very sure, 5= very unsure).

Analysis of *incorrect* versus *correct* but unselected responses showed that physiological measures (systolic blood pressure levels) discriminated *correct*, but unselected response options from *confabulatory* response options. The most salient finding to emerge from this study is that there was a dissociation between behavioral and physiological measures. Physiological measures were able to discriminate confabulations from reality, displaying significantly smaller change in response to correct but unselected response options versus confabulatory response options.

The temporal course of confabulation is well illustrated by the previously mentioned patient with amnesia, who was hospitalized due to a brain aneurysm, and when asked about what she did the night before, talked about traveling to a nearby city and having dinner with her husband. When asked the same question about three weeks later, she responded that she had been in the hospital and never mentioned having dinner with her husband. In other words, the confabulations had resolved, and the information content and temporal context of her retrieval were reasonably accurate.

The neurophysiological correlates associated with her recovery from confabulation are not well understood. But what we do know is that the inner world of unaware phenomena can be accessed using implicit methods, whether behavioral or physiological, so that memories and information associated with reality can be identified although they may not be retrievable via aware and effortful processes.

Chapter 11

When Awareness Interferes with Autonomic Discrimination of Unaware Memory

EEG, functional imaging (i.e., blood flow and oxygenation levels) as well as autonomic discrimination may be able to provide a window through which memories that are unavailable to the processes mediated by conscious and willful retrieval can, nevertheless, be indexed in the absence of awareness. There is an interesting twist, however. Ironically, even a trace of awareness may actually inhibit the operation and expression of the physiological indices of unaware memory expressed by autonomic priming.

For example, in amnesics, "unrecognized" words have been associated with better autonomic discrimination and lower levels of autonomic activity at the encoding stage (Diamond, Mayes & Meudell, 2010). In individuals with a healthy memory and in amnesics who "recognized" a subset of words, encoding tended to be associated with higher levels of autonomic activity and less efficient autonomic priming.

THE INTERACTION OF AWARENESS AND PHYSIOLOGICAL INDICES OF MEMORY IN GREATER DETAIL

This curious interaction reported by Diamond, Mayes and Meudell (2010) demonstrated that in individuals with amnesia, items that were "not-recognized" were associated with better autonomic discrimination and lower levels of physiological activity at encoding. Even among amnesics, some items were recognized, even if only weakly. Interestingly, recognized items were associated with poorer autonomic discrimination and higher levels of physiological activity at encoding. In healthy participants, higher levels of physiological activity at encoding were also associated with better recognition.

In other words, greater EDA activity at encoding was associated with better "explicit" recognition in both amnesics and controls (e.g., Plouffe & Stelmack, 1984) and similar to the ERP (P300) subsequent memory effects reported by Paller et al. (1987). What remains unclear and needs to be demonstrated is whether these effects reflect better elaborative encoding of the studied words and/or their improved consolidation into long-term memory.

In contrast to the amnesic participants, lower levels of activity at encoding in healthy controls were not associated with better autonomic discrimination during recognition trials. In fact, healthy controls generally showed lower levels of autonomic discrimination. A question that has implications for understanding memory in the absence of awareness is why autonomic discrimination among amnesics is better when it is accompanied by lower levels of activity at encoding. This, despite the fact that baseline levels of physiological activity among healthy control subjects and amnesics were comparable.

With respect to possible underlying mechanisms, it may be that while physiological activity and elaborative processing at encoding may have been insufficient to support the elicitation of a conscious and aware sense of familiarity or explicit recognition, the level of activation was sufficient to exceed the threshold for autonomic discrimination. Perhaps the world of unaware phenomena may be more accessible than the world of explicit memories.

Healthy participants do not show this type of response pattern. The answer may be due to the fact that there is a greater response in healthy participants to both old *and* new items. This results in a less differentiated physiological response profile during the recognition phase of the study. Importantly, when differentiating primes from control words, healthy participants may rely on input from both aware (recognition) and unaware (autonomic priming) sources.

A combination of more elaborated encoding and more effective consolidation may result in more fluid and efficient discriminative processing. Greater efficiency generally requires fewer resources and results in lower levels of autonomic activity and a less well-defined and differentiated physiological profile. The degree of stimulus discriminability can also influence physiological activity and may provide additional insight into underlying mechanisms.

For example, Roth (1983), in an experiment using ERPs, reported that greater processing resources were required when discrimination of target from non-target stimuli was more difficult. Differences in stimulus discriminability can elicit different P3 components, in addition to influencing autonomic responsivity (Verbaten, 1983). This may be attributable to the fact that brain regions serving these physiological systems are implicated in memory, in addition to containing afferent and efferent linkages to the autonomic effector system (Frysinger & Harper, 1989).

What do these physiological responses represent? The larger amplitude skin responses and HR decelerative changes from baseline may signify that primes elicited a larger orienting response (Ben-Shakhar, 1994; Boucsein, 1992; Siddle, 1991; Wagner, 1978; Öhman, 1979; Sokolov, 1963) than control words. This is consistent with a model proposed by Lacey and Lacey (1970), suggesting that stimulus intake is associated with heart rate deceleration. Skin responses may be an index of the allocation of attentional resources based on the informational content of the stimulus (Bradley et al., 1990; Lang et al., 1993), reflecting an "implicit" non-emotional learning of associations and contingency rules (Hamm & Vaitl, 1996).

Do skin conductance responses and heart rate activity measure the identical construct? The primary construct that was examined in the Diamond, Mayes and Meudell study was whether electrodermal activity or heart rate showed differential patterns of activity in response to targets that had been primed but remained unrecognized versus control stimuli that had not been primed and were also unrecognized.

Some insight may be derived from a study involving the use of electrodermal and heart rate measures as indices of covert face recognition. Preschoolers have shown increased EDA activity and larger HR decelerative responses to faces that had been previously seen but were *not* recognized (Stormark, 2004). Different physiological responses to primes versus control words may reflect differences in the underlying information content of the stimuli and in the allocation of attentional resources.

The priming process may be expressed differently in amnesics and controls. That is, in amnesics sub-optimal levels of activation may result in poorer encoding and consolidation. In addition, amnesics' impaired explicit recognition may be attributable to damage to the mechanism that mediates feelings of familiarity. Consequently, only a few autonomically discriminated items invoke explicit recognition. This may help contribute to the negative association between autonomic discrimination and recognition among individuals with amnesia.

In healthy controls, the processes underlying familiarity are working normally. Therefore, in healthy individuals, a combination of autonomic discrimination and aware processes co-contribute to achieving recognition, thus showing a positive association. As previously noted, these patterns of findings may be consistent with the state-dependent (e.g., memory) activation-fractionation-inhibition (AFI) model that does provide a framework from which to view and test existing models of episodic memory (Diamond, Mayes & Meudel, 2010).

Therefore, when amnesics do not recognize words, they have been previously exposed to or primed, there is an orienting response to the word that is greater than the orienting response made to unrecognized new words. The OR may be elicited by familiarity or preference (which is independent of recognition) in response to old, unrecognized and recognized items and by a search/checking process that is invoked for recognition and determines whether the word is or is not recognized (Diamond, Mayes & Meudell, 2010).

While previous work has examined the distinct functional and neural substrates underlying encoding and retrieval, this proposed model extends this work by examining the functional relationship between levels of physiological activity at encoding and whether items are subsequently autonomically primed and/or recognized.

The Relationship between Awareness and Autonomic Discrimination

How does one pull all of this together? What does it mean? In order to explain these findings, the state-dependent, activation-fractionation-inhibition model was invoked, which involved an orienting response elicited by preference and search and modulated by underlying memory (Diamond, Mayes & Meudell, 2010). However, simply put, these findings are consistent with the overarching theme of this volume.

That is, despite the fact that patients with amnesia are generally impaired on measures of recognition and recall, they can, under certain conditions, display preserved learning and memory. In order to access unaware memories, tasks need to be structured in such a way that they do not require the elicitation of the context that supported the original learning episode.

Interestingly, in individuals for whom memory was profoundly impaired, memories accessed via unaware and implicit mechanisms was done efficiently and accurately. In contrast, when even weak manifestations of memory emerged, the unaware and implicit mechanisms mediating retrieval were less effective (see Chapter 12, section on Unawareness, Priming and Recognition for more detail).

In order to explore how memory operates in the world of unaware phenomena, future work should manipulate depth of processing at encoding as well as degrade memory at retrieval in healthy individuals. In so doing, we can examine how patterns of physiological priming and recognition can be altered as a function of weaker or stronger memory traces and whether the findings are consistent with the operation of a state-dependent, activation-fractionation–inhibition model.

Predictions about recognition memory strength could also be tested with reaction time protocols (where the response modality is not contaminated by neuropathology) and confidence measures. Generally speaking, controls should be more efficient, faster and more confident about making positive recognition decisions with items judged as having stronger familiarity strengths.

More confident recognition will elicit smaller ORs, and misses will elicit greater ORs, if individuals are unsure about their decision. Also, behavioral priming measures (e.g., category judgment speed) may show greater ORs for behaviorally primed but unrecognized words than for behaviorally unprimed and unrecognized words.

Additionally, future work can also use brain imaging and autonomic monitoring in order to examine the relationship between levels of activity at encoding and patterns of activity at retrieval for primed and/or recognized items and determine where these processes are represented in the brain, providing additional insight into whether these measures reflect distinct and dissociable memory systems. Work also needs to examine the two triggers (i.e., preference and the search/checking process) separately, in order to confirm that healthy controls and amnesics have an equal number of primed memories.

Chapter 12

Preserved and Impaired
Implicit Learning in Amnesia

Amnesics have shown preserved learning on a number of tasks including classical conditioning (Daum, Channon, & Canavan, 1989, but see Myers et al., 2001); pursuit rotor (Cohen, 1984); and skill-based learning (i.e., reading mirror reversed words) (Mishkin, Malamut, & Bachevalier, 1984).

These findings are, however, a bit more nuanced. That is, while individuals with mesial temporal (MT) amnesia display spared delay eyeblink classical conditioning (EBCC), amnestic individuals with aneurysms affecting the anterior communicating artery (ACoA) which involves the basal forebrain (BF) region, show impairment at delay EBCC (Myers et al., 2002). Thus, a caveat that should be emphasized is that some conditioning tasks may involve information that is organized and stored in brain regions that differ from where those memory representations impaired in amnesia are generally believed to be stored and processed.

By implication, these findings suggest that the specific brain regions affected in amnesia influence whether certain types of conditioning and learning are spared or impaired. Moreover, these findings have implications for the world of unaware phenomena as they provide additional evidence supporting the distinction and dissociations between implicit memory (i.e., no reference to a previous learning episode) and explicit memory (i.e., where judgments are made about whether a test stimulus was previously encountered in a particular spatiotemporal context) supporting dissociable memory processes and neural substrates (Wagner & Gabrieli, 1998).

UNAWARENESS, PRIMING AND RECOGNITION:
IMPLICATIONS FOR ILLUMINATING UNAWARENESS

What is the relationship between unawareness, priming and recognition? To begin with, recognition memory has been viewed from a variety of theoretical perspectives including single and dual-process models (Curran, DeBuse, Woroch, & Hirshman, 2006). Single process models view recognition memory as distributed along a continuum with memory strength ranging from weak to strong. Dual process models view recognition memory as comprised of recollection and familiarity.

Familiarity is generally viewed as an unconscious or automatic process whereas recollection is mediated by conscious, willful and effortful processing (Jacoby,1991). From the perspective of a dual-process model, recollection reflects a threshold process whereby qualitative information is retrieved about a study event. Whereas familiarity is generally characterized as reflecting a signal detection process.

In an individual, items that exceed a familiarity threshold are thought by that person to have been previously studied. Individuals with amnesia, despite having been previously exposed to items, may report that none of the items were previously studied based on the fact that the items did not exceed a putative familiarity threshold or the conscious awareness of having exceeded that threshold. Recollection and familiarity are viewed as separate and distinct memory retrieval processes (Yonelinas, 2001).

If a stimulus falls below either threshold, it will likely not induce either recollection or a sense of familiarity but it may produce a weak and perhaps not even perceptible sense of familiarity or awareness. However, it may bias decision-making in favor of an unrecollected and unfamiliar stimulus.

In other words, this is an example of a memory about which an individual is unaware but nevertheless it influences decision-making in the absence of any clear and discernible sense of familiarity or recollection. One might wonder how many of the decisions in our lives are influenced by memories or associations about which we are unaware but nevertheless can alter the direction of our lives, our choices, our likes and dislikes.

Repetition Priming and Physiological
Correlates of Unaware Memory

Similarly, there is evidence suggesting that repetition priming, which is a form of implicit memory, in which there is a biasing of a response, or an enhancement of the fluency of item-specific processing as a function of prior exposure to that item is generally preserved in amnesics (Jacoby & Kelley,

1994). This is relevant to the overarching theme of this text as this response bias occurs in the absence of any awareness of prior exposure to the item but behavioral and physiological measures (e.g., Electrodermal Activity [EDA]) that have been used as indices of priming can show a distinct bias in favor of the previously experienced item or stimulus

There are varying perspectives regarding the mechanism(s) underlying priming. For example, Schacter (1987) proposed that priming in amnesics is based on the transitory activation of premorbid memory traces. However, it is also thought that priming may be based on faster processing of remembered items (Reinitz & Alexander, 1996); items not consciously remembered but for which an individual had prior exposure or presumably on the basis of automatic access to episodic memories that result in enhanced item fluency (Jacoby & Kelley, 1994). In addition, there is also evidence that enhanced item fluency can last for considerable periods of time (see Mayes, 1988).

So, taken together, while amnesics display levels of recognition that are not much better than chance, they can exhibit priming at normal levels. In other words, they exhibit a preference for previously studied versus unstudied stimuli, in the absence of conscious recognition of the stimuli (Squire & McKee, 1992). Moreover, preserved priming has been displayed not only for familiar verbal information (Shimamura, 1986), but also for familiar non-verbal information (Paller et al., 1992).

Given that both autonomic measures (i.e., EDA) and event related potentials (ERPs) have been used as indices of priming, what do these physiological measures signify? With respect to EDA responses, it appears that they are associated with the orienting response to novel stimuli (Ben-Shakhar, 1994; Siddle, 1991). In fact, most cognitive and motor activities are accompanied by skin conductance responses (SCRs) (Boucsein, 1992). It has been posited that the EDA may represent an index of attentional resource allocation that depends on informational content, rather than on the emotional qualities of the stimulus (Bradley et al., 1990; Lang et al., 1993).

The body of evidence supporting the findings that autonomic measures can index memory in the absence of awareness continues to grow. Tranel, Fowles and Damasio (1985) found that EDA in healthy people could index responses that differentiate familiar versus unfamiliar faces with familiar faces evoking larger amplitude responses.

Similar findings have been reported in prosopagnosia, where more frequent, consistent and significantly greater amplitude skin responses are found in response to familiar versus unfamiliar faces (Tranel & Damasio, 1985) and to correct versus incorrect face-name matches (Bauer, 1984).

Verfaellie, Bauer and Bowers (1991) reported that TR, an amnesic patient showed poor recognition of words when tested at a delay of 30 minutes. However, when memory was indexed by EDA activity TR showed more normal memory. In another example, EDA activity in a 63-year-old male patient with frontal lobe damage was monitored while performing a familiarity decision task using familiar and unfamiliar faces. While producing significantly more overt false recognition errors (false positives) and misidentifications (misses) in response to unfamiliar faces, this patient showed accurate covert autonomic discrimination of familiar versus unfamiliar faces (Rapcsak et al., 1998).

Unaware memory or covert recognition, as previously demonstrated, has been indexed using a variety of physiological measures. For example, the P300 component of the ERP has also been used, in the context of the oddball paradigm, revealing that the P300 amplitude was larger in a prosopagnosic patient in response to faces that should have evoked a sense of familiarity but did not (Renault, Signoret, Debruille, Breton, & Bolgert, 1989). P300s elicited by repeated words tend to be more positive-going than for new words, while P300s elicited by words repeated once are smaller than for words repeated twice, but greater than for new stimuli. These findings may reflect differential sensitivity to the variable strength of the underlying memory trace (Bentin & Moscovitch, 1990).

Relatedly, Diamond, Mayes and Meudell (1996) reported that in a group of amnesics of mixed etiology, priming (indexed by levels of autonomic discrimination) in response to previously studied, but unrecognized words versus words that had not been studied previously, did not significantly differ from levels of recognition in a healthy control group. Moreover, these findings appeared to suggest that autonomic discrimination tended to be better in patients who exhibited more impaired recognition.

Chapter 13

Implicit Bias, Executive Control, Brain Metabolism and Processing Speed

Bias can be expressed in a variety of ways. It can be manifested explicitly, in behaviors, in actions and attitudes but often bias can remain hidden or submerged, unknown to others and, sometimes, even unknown to the individual in whom it is expressed. Executive control processes have been identified as possible mediators that influence the expression or suppression of prejudicial thought and behavior (e.g., Payne, 2005; Richeson et al., 2003). It has been proposed that individuals with high or low executive control may have the same experience of bias, but those with poor executive control are more likely to be perceived or behave in prejudicial ways (Payne, 2005).

The Implicit Association Test (IAT) (Greenwald, McGhee, & Schwartz, 1998) has, over the last several decades, been used as a measure of implicit bias. The IAT is an association-based test that measures disparities in millisecond reaction time or latencies in response to various conditions. For example, the speed with which a participant associates pleasant (i.e., happiness) or unpleasant (i.e., crime) with categories, such as, "black" or "white," "male" or "female" is measured.

Implicit attitudes have been assessed in response to socially neutral categories, such as flower versus insect, and images representing these categories are paired with pleasant versus unpleasant words. The procedure involves instructing test takers to first hit the "positive" key when a flower appears on the computer screen; hit the "negative" key when insects appear and hit the "positive" key when pleasant words appear and hit the "negative" key when unpleasant words appear. The procedure then entails switching the flowers/insect categories and instructs test takers to create "incompatible" pairings. Thus, participants are then instructed to select the "positive" key when insects or pleasant words appear but select the "negative" key when flowers or unpleasant words appear.

The underlying logic of the procedure is affirmed by the extant IAT research literature that reports that stronger associations are formed when combinations are compatible. Reaction time latencies in milliseconds are used as an index of the strength of the association between combinations that are compatible versus those that are not. Thus, pictures of flowers (e.g., a rose or tulip) combined with pleasant words and pictures of insects (e.g., a wasp or horsefly) combined with unpleasant words produced faster reaction times than the incompatible pairing of flowers and unpleasant words or insects and pleasant words.

The IAT methodology has also been used to evaluate implicit racial bias. Therefore, in "compatible" conditions, test takers are instructed to select the "positive" key when white pictures and pleasant words appear, and to hit the "negative" key when black pictures and unpleasant words appear.

For the "incompatible" set of pairings, test takers are told to hit the "positive" key when black pictures and pleasant words appeared and to hit the "negative" key when white pictures and unpleasant words appeared on the screen. These various combinations produce differential response times indicating that, on average, the "compatible" pairings generated faster reaction times than the "incompatible" combinations.

These findings have been used as evidence supporting the idea that the differences in millisecond reaction time demonstrated unconscious racism. For example, blacks paired with unpleasant words resulted in faster response times than blacks paired with pleasant words, while whites paired with pleasant words resulted in faster response times than whites paired with unpleasant words. It should be emphasized that processing and accompanying response latency differentials occur in the absence of conscious awareness of racial bias. Thus, the world of unaware phenomena once again emerges and appears to find expression in yet another way and context.

The IAT's underlying construct and methodology have been the subject of controversy with some reports indicating that the IAT may confound method variance that is associated with executive control with the construct of prejudice (e.g., Klauer, Schmitz, Teige-Mocigemba, & Voss, 2010; Mierke & Klauer, 2001; see also Nosek, Greenwald, & Banaji, 2007).

Various models have been proposed in order to conceptualize the relationships between bias, awareness and executive control mechanisms. These relationships have been viewed through the lens of controlled versus automatic processing (Hasher & Zacks, 1979) as well as Dual-Process models (e.g., Wilson, Lindsey, & Schooler, 2000) that view overt behavior as largely driven by aware, intentional and controlled processes. Generally, it is theorized that implicit processes control automatic reactions and nonverbal behaviors and associations (e.g., Dovidio et al., 2002; Knutson, Wood, Spampinato, & Grafman, 2006; McConnel & Liebold, 2001).

Group evaluations and interracial interactions are also thought to be modulated by executive control processes and motivation (Legault, Green-Demers, Grant, Chung, 2007; Payne, 2005; Richeson et al., 2003). Bias, when manifested as an unaware phenomenon, has been viewed from the perspective that automatic activation and suppression or compensation for bias are unconsciously monitored (Glaser & Kihlstrom, 2005) by executive control processes.

In order to evaluate the precise role of executive control functions in mediating these relationships, *process dissociation procedures* (Payne, 2005) have been implemented. Generally, findings derived from this research suggest that executive ability and motivation for an individual to appear unbiased are directly related to the magnitude of executive control exerted on an implicit priming task.

In other words, individuals with more efficient executive control functions are more competent in controlling the expression of behaviors thought to reflect *automatic* underlying biases, so that executive control is inversely related to the expression of prejudice (Correll et al., 2007).

PHYSIOLOGICAL CORRELATES OF BIAS

In addition to behavioral measures, a variety of physiological measures and techniques have also been used to examine the expression of implicit and explicit bias. For example, implicit and explicit measures of racial bias have been differentially expressed in the contingent negative variation (CNV) component of the event-related potential (ERP) (Chiu, Ambady, & Deldin, 2004), in activation of the amygdala (Cunningham et al., 2004; Phelps et al., 2000) and in patterns of prefrontal cortex (PFC) activation (Amodio, Harmon-Jones, Devine, Curtin, & Covert, 2004; Knutson et al., 2006).

Recent investigations suggest that the operation of these neural substrates may underlie automatic evaluative processing (Cunningham et al., 2004; Phelps, Cannistraci, & Cunningham, 2003) and support the role of the amygdala in social group evaluative processes (Hart, 2000). For example, higher levels of implicit bias are associated with greater amygdala activity in response to viewing African American faces (Cunningham et al., 2004; Phelps et al., 2000). Notably, the amygdala activation is occurring in the absence of any conscious awareness of either the bias or the increased activation.

Converging lines of evidence suggest a role for the anterior cingulate cortex (ACC) of the prefrontal cortex (PFC) in ethnic-group evaluative processes (Amodio et al., 2004). The PFC putatively acts as an area that reflects individual differences in the strength and focus of attentional control mechanisms mediated via thalamic gating and serving controlled versus automatic processing (Barrett, 2004). Taken together, both emotional and executive control centers may be activated during both implicit and explicit expressions of prejudice.

With respect to the temporal processing characteristics of these control centers, there is evidence that activity in the ACC and dorsolateral PFC (which modulate "automatic" amygdala-mediated responses) may be invoked very early on when making racial evaluations (Cunningham et al., 2004). Early CNV amplitudes, generated in response to cues that signaled the presentation of African American faces with angry expressions, have been interpreted by some investigators as reflecting the anticipation of cognitive effort to control racial bias (Chiu et al., 2004).

The fact that these mechanisms may operate outside of the individuals' conscious awareness (Glaser & Kihlstrom, 1999) is relevant to the world of unaware phenomena. Moreover, because of modulation of the fluency of cognitive processing, response latencies on implicit tasks may result in larger or smaller latencies as a function of additional processing and/or the activation of neural networks that are more or less salient (Amodio et al., 2004; Cunningham et al., 2004).

Thus, what has been characterized as the *IAT effect* has been defined as the difference in latency between trials that pair congruent stimuli (congruent condition) and trials that pair non-congruent stimuli (non-congruent condition) with latencies that are log transformed before computing the average difference between conditions (Greenwald, McGhee, & Schwartz, 1998). From a methodological perspective, in order to eliminate or reduce the effects of general processing speed, the *D* measure transformation was developed. It involves dividing the latency difference between conditions by the standard deviation of latency scores (pooled from both conditions) (Greenwald, Nosek, & Banaji, 2003). However, the log transformation measure is still thought by some to produce a substantial amount of method variance associated with processing speed (Klauer et al., 2010) as does the *D* measure (Blanton & Jaccard, 2006).

It has been suggested that the underlying mechanisms that govern the expression of implicit bias may be influenced by executive control mechanisms and processing speed, so that greater executive control and processing speed would be inversely related to implicit measures of racial bias. In other words, greater speed and better executive control would be associated with lower levels of implicit bias. The use of multiple measures of processing speed with varying levels of executive demand would enhance the methodology underlying the use of implicit measures in evaluating relationships between processing speed and implicit bias.

Information Processing Speed and Bias

In a study involving 51 European American adults, ranging in age from 19 to 55, the relationship between processing speed and Implicit Association Test (IAT) performance was examined using a race and a socially neutral IAT. Simple reaction time was *not* correlated with IAT performance. However, it was reported that faster higher-level processing speed on a 3-back task was correlated with lower transformed scores and shorter latencies on implicit association race and neutral measures (Diamond et al., 2012).

In other words, faster processing speed was associated with lower levels of implicit bias perhaps suggesting that higher-level processing and measures of implicit bias may be mediated, in part, by shared executive control processes. In fact, higher-level processing may account for approximately 70 percent of this relationship with general processing speed accounting for the remainder.

Higher-level processing and the mechanisms that mitigate the expression of implicit bias may, at least in part, be mediated by shared executive processes whereby individuals with lower implicit bias exhibit more efficient executive control resulting in faster higher-level processing and in appearing or being less biased.

Similarly, individuals with race and neutral IAT D scores at or below the twenty-fifth percentile (i.e., lower implicit bias) displayed faster processing on the 3-back task than individuals with D scores at the seventy-fifth percentile (i.e., higher implicit bias). In other words, smaller race and neutral IAT latencies were associated with faster processing on the 3-back task. The latency differentials between compatible conditions (European Americans paired with pleasant words and African Americans paired with unpleasant words) and incompatible conditions (European Americans paired with unpleasant words and African Americans paired with pleasant words) were not related to dual task processing speed. However, Dual Task processing speed was correlated with compatible condition latencies.

So, what does all of this mean with respect to the world of unaware phenomena? Faster processing is thought to be associated with the mapping of stereotypically compatible concepts onto single responses. If, over time, we have associated whites with positive words, images and concepts and blacks with negative words, images and concepts, these response patterns and associations will have been learned and reinforced over the course of a lifetime and result in more rapid and efficient processing.

Conversely, if Blacks are associated with positive words, images and concepts, it is postulated that in individuals with implicit bias their processing of these associations will be slower and less efficient because they not as well learned and have not been reinforced.

The association between dual task performance and compatible latencies may be based on the idea that these latencies indicate automatic associations that more closely reflect the recruitment of executive functions underlying the processing of compatible conditions. Speed alone, however, did not account for the entirety of these relationships, as simple reaction time was not correlated with any of the race or socially neutral IAT measures. Partial correlations suggested that higher-level processing may account for about 69 percent of the processing speed-latency relationship in the race and a slightly lower value (approximately 66%) in the socially neutral task.

In other words, the latencies on implicit bias measures were correlated with higher-level processing speed tasks that required varying levels of executive control. How does it relate to unawareness? Implicit bias measures purport show bias in individuals who may be totally unaware of such bias. Better performance on the higher-level information processing measures appears to reflect executive control efficiencies that mitigate implicit bias and conversely slower higher-level information processing is associated with higher levels of implicit bias.

Patterns of everyday neurobehavioral engagement, activation and reaction may reflect the information efficiency of the individual. This may suggest that in individuals with lower implicit bias, executive processes may be more efficient resulting in faster higher-level processing and thus appearing to be less biased. In many instances, bias and prejudice may be beyond our awareness and only emerges via implicit method. However, it appears as if differences in executive control and processing speed may influence the expression of implicit and explicit bias, thus an individual may appear to be less biased or may, in fact, be less biased.

Racial Bias and Brain Blood Oxygen Levels

Functional imaging techniques have also provided insight into the inner workings of unaware phenomena particularly with respect to racial bias. That is, individuals exhibiting lower levels of implicit bias show lower levels of activation in regions that have been implicated in processing faces of African Americans (e.g., dorsolateral prefrontal cortex, anterior cingulate cortex and amygdala).

This is in contrast to the finding that higher levels of implicit bias may be associated with greater allocation of resources and more extensive activation of neural regions resulting in the depletion of executive resources (Richeson et al., 2004).

The underlying premise of resource depletion is that an increased allocation of resources would result in a depletion of executive resources that would then contribute to a decrease in the efficiency of executive control processes for coping with bias-evoking stimuli (Richeson et al., 2004). What is both interesting and relevant to the theme of unawareness is that these processes are presumably operating on an unaware level. Thus, individuals who are more efficient in executive function, processing speed (Blanton & Jaccard, 2006) and set-switching abilities (Mierke & Klauer, 2001) are more likely to be classified as less prejudiced and perform in less biased ways on socially neutral tasks as well.

In addition, individuals who exhibit less extensive activation and engage fewer resources during processing of African American faces exhibit more efficient executive control and faster processing on higher-order tasks. With the engagement of fewer resources they are also less likely to exhibit resource depletion. If the location and degree of activation provide insight into efficiency, then in addition to the IAT, functional imaging may also be able to provide a window into the neural substrates underlying the processing of race-related stimuli, thus potentially serving as both an index of activation and engagement that occur on an unaware level.

What is most relevant to our exploration of unawareness is that neural processes, networks and associations are operating and influencing behavior in ways about which we are unaware. Brain and autonomic nervous system function may also be modified by biased and prejudicial beliefs, feelings, and attitudes on an unaware level. The exception of course, is when they are given expression using implicit behavioral measures (i.e., IAT) or indexed by physiological markers (e.g., autonomic, event related potentials [ERP] or blood flow and oxygenation levels).

It appears as though the relationship between higher-level executive processing speed and implicit bias (e.g., *D*, latency and latency difference scores) is expressed as a combination of general (Blanton, Jacquard, Gonzalez & Christy, 2006) and higher-level processing speed with the higher-level component sensitive to differences in the efficiency of executive control and a less responsive and relatively undifferentiated processing speed component.

With respect to future research, developing an IAT implicit bias transformation that corrects for the relative contributions of higher-level and general processing speed would be helpful. Future research also needs to examine how baseline executive processing efficiency, implicit measure construction and, perhaps, automatic cognitive-physiological reaction patterns, interact in ways that may support faster executive processing speed in individuals with lower implicit bias.

Memories and circuits can be accessed on an unaware level and these internal processes impact our decision-making, our everyday lives and social justice issues as well. These implicit measures, to some degree, help penetrate the veil of unawareness that shrouds so much of our existence and a substantial portion of our behaviors.

On a clinical and philosophical level, if we remain unaware of what we think and how we feel, we are not able to self-evaluate and reflect on our lives with any accuracy and, thus we may be unable to meaningfully change or modify our behaviors and attitudes. In this case, the world of unawareness could perpetuate bias and inequities that diminish the richness of all of our lives and affect some groups adversely and disproportionately.

Skill and Computer Learning, Preferences, and Unaware Phenomena

The way in which implicit memories are accessed and the nature of the target information can influence the duration of priming in amnestic patients. How is this manifested and why does it matter? In skill learning, unawareness of the learning context or an inability to explicitly retrieve that information does not mean that the information cannot influence behavior.

For example, amnesics can exhibit acquired preferences for previously heard melodies (Johnson, Kim & Riss, 1985) and they can find a hidden figure more rapidly after only a single exposure (Crovitz, Harvey & McClanahan, 1979). The densely amnesic patient HM could acquire motor skills as evidenced by his performance in the pursuit rotor and mirror tracing tasks (Milner, Corkin & Teuber, 1968). This was demonstrated despite the fact that HM did not explicitly remember having previously performed the task. In other words, a previous skill-based experience influenced his later performance in the absence of any explicit awareness or memory of the prior learning episode.

From the perspective of procedural memory theory, skill learning is viewed as dependent on a procedural memory system that based on a substantial literature appears to be spared in amnesic patients. However, this system does not support explicit remembering. The strength of this view is that it provides a reasonably straightforward account of *normal* perceptual-motor skill learning in amnesics who lack conscious recollection of prior episodes.

If we do not probe and use the implicit retrieval techniques available to us, we will not be able to reconstruct the memories and associations that have been encoded and stored within individuals who cannot explicitly retrieve that information. In essence, portions of people's lives and experiences will remain unknown and inaccessible. The implicit retrieval techniques have broad implications for a variety of areas including but not restricted to therapeutic, educational and forensic interventions.

McAndrews, Glisky, and Schacter (1987) reported that even severely amnesic patients show strong priming effects on a sentence puzzle task, Moreover, the effect was durable and was demonstrated after a retention interval of one week. Importantly, Glisky, Schacter and Tulving (1986) demonstrated that a densely amnesic patient could learn how to program a computer, which in and of itself is notable. However, what is even more intriguing is that this learning occurred in the absence of any explicit awareness that the patient had ever worked on a computer.

This finding indicated that patients with profound memory disorders can acquire and retain the complex knowledge needed to learn and apply the procedures integral to computer programming. Densely amnesic patient C.H., who retained no conscious memory of his computer experiences, could learn to write and edit simple programs and was able to perform select computer operations.

A patient with memory impairments secondary to viral encephalitis and who was severely impaired on standardized tests of verbal and non-verbal memory, displayed learning when materials were presented using the vanishing cues procedure. The vanishing cues procedure was designed specifically to tap patients' preserved abilities to produce recently presented words in the presence of fragment cues, as shown in research on direct priming. The patient did acquire new knowledge and she was able to apply it and she retained learning with very little forgetting over a seven-month time period.

However, it is acknowledged that while patients were able to attain performance levels that were quantitatively equivalent to those of controls, learning was not normal and required multiple repetitions before error-free learning was achieved. The learning was also characterized as qualitatively different versus controls.

Importantly, individuals with dense amnesia exhibited memory and priming for information and puzzles in the absence of conscious awareness. Moreover, despite the fact that amnesics cannot tell you where, how or when they learned how to use the computer, the world of unaware memory and learning emerged and was expressed in ways that allowed patients to use computers in a functional manner.

Chapter 14

Methods and Models for Examining Unaware Phenomena in the Brain

Neurobehavioral, Computer-Based, Neuroimaging and Autonomic

IMPLICIT BEHAVIORAL MEASURES

Implicit behavioral measures (e.g., IAT) and physiological indices, such as fMRI (Richeson et al., 2003) may also provide insight into prejudice and anxiety, although aspects of this research remain controversial (see chapter 13). Implicit effects have been indexed through priming, response bias, preference, perceptual facilitation, changes in brain activation and autonomic nervous system function (Diamond, Mayes & Meudell, 1996; Schacter, Dobbins, & Schnyer, 2004).

Neurobehavioral Correlates of Unaware Memory

While individuals with amnesia often exhibit profound impairments on a variety of measures of recognition and recall, they can, nevertheless, display preserved short-term memory on the digit span task and exhibit normal recency effects in tasks involving free recall (Cermak & Stiassny, 1982; Baddeley, 1982). Moreover, amnesiacs show learning and retention for motor skills as observed on the pursuit rotor task (Cohen, 1984) and they also exhibit preserved perceptual skill learning (i.e., learning to read mirror reversed words) (Cohen & Squire, 1980) despite the fact that they may not remember the initial learning episode or context in which the learning has taken place.

Perceptual Skill Learning and Conditioning

Classical conditioning also appears to be preserved in amnesiacs (Weiskrantz & Warrington, 1979; Daum et al., 1989; Myers et al., 2001). There is a caveat, however. Classical conditioning may be largely mediated by the cerebellum (Lye et al., 1988) and the basal ganglia are implicated in skill and habit formation (Mishkin, Malamut & Bachevalier, 1984). Thus, memories for these types of information may be both organized and stored in neural regions that differ from the information largely processed and stored in the neocortical regions of individuals with amnesia.

Item-Specific Implicit Memory: Priming

There is a type of item-specific implicit memory, whereby behavioral responses may be influenced and biased as a function of prior exposure to an item, but in the absence of any explicit memory for the context in which the original learning took place. This type of memory is called priming and a body of work has provided evidence suggesting that it is preserved in amnesia. Moreover, it may be processed, stored and organized in the association neocortical regions similar to the kinds of memory that are impaired in amnesia (Diamond, Mayes & Meudell, 1996). Evidence supports the idea that preserved priming may extend to both familiar verbal (Shimamura, 1986) and non-verbal information (Paller, Mayes & Thompson et al., 1992). What needs to be emphasized is that priming can occur in the absence of conscious recall and recognition.

Verbal Information

Preserved item-specific implicit memory and priming have been demonstrated on a wide range of tasks including stem completion paradigms where there is a response bias in the direction of the rarer form of the word. Moreover, the strength of this effect is similar to that observed in controls (Shimamura, 1986; Jacoby and Witherspoon, 1982). Item-specific priming has been demonstrated in spelling orally presented homophones and on free association tasks in response to the first word in each word pair following exposure to related word pairs (e.g., soldier-rifle) (Shimamura & Squire, 1984; Mayes, Pickering & Fairbairn, 1987).

Priming has also been shown in paradigms where prior exposure to a word facilitates subsequent identification of that word under degraded viewing conditions (i.e., under conditions where words are presented very briefly) (Jacoby & Dallas, 1981; Cermak , 1985). It appears that word identification is below the threshold for conscious recognition and that subsequent identification of the word occurs in the absence of any conscious recall of the word's prior exposure. In a similar vein, learning a repeating sequence of verbal stimuli can occur without awareness, but only when the stimulus response mapping required an attention-demanding activity (Hartman, Knopman & Nissen, 1989).

Physiological Indices of Unaware Memory: Event-Related Potentials (ERPs) and Autonomic Correlates

Memory in the absence of awareness has also been demonstrated using physiological measures in both healthy and clinical populations. For example, event-related potentials (ERPs) have provided evidence of covert discrimination of faces for which no conscious recognition had been demonstrated. Using an oddball paradigm, Renault et al. (1989) found that the P300 ERP amplitude was larger in response to famous faces (rare events) that should have been familiar but were not recognized. In the second condition of this experiment, unfamiliar and familiar faces occurred with equiprobability and in contrast to condition one, the P300 amplitude did not vary as a function of stimulus category.

Bentin and Moscovitch (1990) using words of average frequency in semantic and lexical decision tasks found that at testing (delay of five minutes), P300s elicited by repeated words were more positive than for new words. In the next stage of the study, in what was characterized as an "implicit" test, P300s elicited in response to presentation of "new" words were smaller than P300s elicited by "old" words. Moreover, there was a titration effect. In other words, P300s elicited by words that were repeated once were smaller than for words repeated twice, but greater than for new stimuli. It has been proposed that P300 amplitude may reflect the strength of a memory trace and that the strength of the memory representation varies as a function of the number of word repetitions and the recency of the stimulus repetition (see Onofrj et al., 1991).

Intact measures of implicit memory from 400 to 600 ms post stimulus onset have been reported in a group of mild amnesia patients with evidence of MTL damage limited to the hippocampus during a test of item recognition confidence during electroencephalogram (EEG) acquisition. Using a procedure that eliminated declarative memory differences, the authors re-analyzed the data to study event related potentials (ERPs) of implicit memory and reported reliable implicit memory effects in posterior scalp regions from 400 to 600 ms which was topographically dissociated from the explicit memory effects of familiarity. Patients were found to be impaired in implicit memory effects relative to control subjects. Although implicit and explicit effects were topographically dissociated, both the implicit and explicit memory system appeared to rely upon the same neural structures but they functioned in what was characterized as different physiological ways. Thus, there is some evidence that the hippocampus plays a role in aspects of memory processing that are presumably beyond the realm of conscious awareness (Addante, 2015).

In addition to behavioral, perceptual and ERP-based measures that have indexed memory in the absence of awareness, biased responses to specific items as a result of having previously experienced the item and in the absence of conscious awareness of the previous exposure have also been demonstrated using autonomic measures.

For example, subjects have displayed accurate electrodermal responses (EDR) to target stimuli even when stimuli were degraded or camouflaged so that identification was made more difficult (Lazarus & McLeary, 1951; Corteen & Wood, 1972). Rousey and Holzman (1967) reported larger EDR responses in subjects who heard their own voice irrespective of whether they did or did not recognize it as their own voice. Individuals exposed to randomly generated geometric shapes for one millisecond later displayed a preference for and larger EDR responses to the "old" versus the "new" stimuli. This occurred despite the fact that recognition was no better than chance (Kunst-Wilson & Zajonc, 1979). Tranel, Fowles and Damasio (1985) reported that larger amplitude skin responses were evoked by familiar versus unfamiliar faces.

Similar effects have been demonstrated in prosopagnosics despite their severely compromised ability to recognize faces that should have been familiar (Bauer, 1984; Tranel & Damasio, 1985). Larger skin conductance responses, one week following learning, were reported for "old" versus "new" neutral and emotionally laden words (Rees-Nishio & Moscovitch, 1985).

Verfaellie, Bauer and Bowers (1991) similarly report the case of a 39-year-old, college-educated accountant, TR. TR was severely amnesic due to a left retrosplenial-fornix lesion and was presented with a learning task involving 32 visually presented words. When tested at a delay of 30 minutes, TR recognized 44 percent of the targets which was significantly worse than controls, who on average recognized 91 percent of the targets. However, despite impaired recognition, TR did show "more normal" discriminative recognition using electrodermal measures.

Diamond, Mayes and Meudell (1997) examined autonomic and recognition indices of memory in six amnesic subjects of mixed etiology and six control subjects, all of whom were matched with respect to age, education and intelligence. Despite showing impaired recognition, amnesics displayed significantly better autonomic discrimination of previously experienced targets. Moreover, the level of autonomic discrimination displayed by amnesics did not significantly differ from healthy control subjects' level of recognition.

The autonomic measures were expressed as orienting-type responses and appeared to be differentially sensitive in amnesics and controls. That is, EDR measures were greater in amplitude and heart rate was decelerative in response to targets, across both amnesics and controls. However, heart rate tended to be a more sensitive measure in controls, whereas skin response was a more sensitive measure among amnesics.

In addition, amnesics displayed levels of confidence in false alarms and hits that did not significantly differ, which is in sharp contrast to the significantly greater levels of confidence expressed by healthy controls in hits versus false alarms. Basically, amnesics' inaccurate confidence reflects the lack of, or significantly reduced, internal feedback that would be differentially evoked in response to hits and false alarms as seen in controls. The issue of whether the level of electrophysiologically indexed recognition is fully preserved compared with healthy controls remains unresolved. Importantly, in the aforementioned studies the inner world of nonconscious or unaware memory was accessed via behavioral and physiological indices and manifested as larger amplitude electrodermal and ERP responses.

PET: Positron Emission Tomography

A variety of tools, techniques and methodologies have been used to access the world of unaware phenomena. However, in many instances, these techniques require complex technologies to record physiological events and to analyze and interpret data. PET imaging, like fMRI, is based on the finding that areas of the brain that are more active have increased blood flow due to increased neuronal activity. Active brain regions consume more resources, in the form of oxygen or glucose, with these nutrients ultimately transported throughout the brain via blood flow. PET imaging detects changes in the brain's blood flow by measuring changes in oxygen or glucose utilization (Raichle & Posner, 1997).

The theoretical basis for PET technology was laid out by the 1943 Nobel Laureate George de Hevesy (Jones & Townsend, 2017) "for his work on the use of isotopes as tracers in the study of chemical processes" (Nobelprize. org). PET detects the decay of radiochemicals and a significant strength of this methodology is the vast number of substances that can be labeled with radioisotopes including glucose, oxygen, neurotransmitters, pH, amino acids, and proteins (Jones & Townsend, 2017).

PET arguably has the greatest specificity and sensitivity in imaging at the molecular level (Jones & Townsend, 2017). Pet scanners have been in use since the 1960s, but those early scanners were of limited utility, as they had only single pairs of detectors and could cover only a limited part of the body (about 25 cm), detecting in only a single, 2-dimensional plane. Currently, multi-ring scanners are the norm. The most advanced PET scanner, originally conceptualized by Badawi and Cherry in 2011, is the whole-body EXPLORER which has 560 individual detector elements and can image the entire body (axial length of 2 m), mapping out the movement of the radiopharmaceutical as it courses through the body in real time (Cherry et al., 2017).

PET: Overview

The photon-detecting scanner is a donut-shaped device in which participants are positioned. The participant is injected with a small amount of radioactive water; for example with the radioactive isotope Oxygen-15 or 2-deoxy-2-(^{18}F)fluoro-D-glucose, both these radiopharmaceuticals are highly unstable with a very short half-life and as a result must be prepared in a cyclotron very near the PET scanner. The fact that the creation of radioactive isotopes must happen in close proximity to the scanner is one of the major rate-limiting steps with respect to accessibility to PET imaging technology.

Electrons with a positive charge, or positrons, are emitted from the radiopharmaceutical due to their highly unstable chemical nature. These positrons are attracted to the negatively charged electrons within the body and the meeting of the two causes a collision, annihilating both the positron and electron and releasing small amounts of energy in the form of two photons per collision. The photons leave the body at the opposite side to the original collision and as they leave, the donut-shaped photon detectors (PET camera) that comprise the PET scanning machine in which the participant lays resting, can detect them.

As the photons exit at opposite sides, the distance travelled varies, hence the time it takes to reach the photon camera also varies and this differential in timing is used to locate the annihilation source and then can determine the exact location of the event in 3-dimensional space. Reconstruction algorithms are applied to produce the images of variations of blood flow activity. Like the advances in PET scanning technology, the algorithms have also undergone refinement allowing for more accurate reconstruction (Defrise, Kinahan & Michel, 2003).

PET Research and Implicit Processes

One of the early PET studies that looked at the neuroanatomical substrates of priming (stem completion) in a memory task was conducted by Buckner et al. (1995). They found the expected faster performance in the priming versus the baseline condition, and that overall patterns of cortical activation were highly similar in both conditions. An interesting finding in the priming condition was a decrease in neuronal activity in occipital-temporal areas which was greater on the right than the left side. Buckner et al. (1995) interpreted these results as an indicator of greater processing efficiency for the primed words versus the baseline conditions. In other words, priming based on prior word exposure was expressed as a decrease in neuronal activity which was interpreted as indicating more efficient or fluent processing.

Serial Reaction Time Task

Evidence of prior learning or exposure has also been demonstrated in the context of the serial reaction time task, an implicit motor task originally developed by Nissen and Bullemer (1987). The task consists of participants pressing one of four buttons in response to targets appearing at specific locations on a computer monitor; locations can be recurring or random sequences. Participants who were not informed that there may be recurring sequences exhibited decreased response times for the recurring sequences.

This task, although thought to be a measure of implicit serial motor (procedural) learning, is also arguably a much richer, more complex behavioral measure (Robertson, 2007). Rauch et al. (1997) utilized the serial reaction time task to compare implicit sequence learning in a group of nine female patients diagnosed with obsessive-compulsive disorder (OCD) to nine healthy female controls. As with most neuroimaging studies using complex imaging techniques, such as PET, the sample size is smaller than for behavioral research paradigms and thus research generalizations need to be interpreted cautiously.

The corticostriatal system has been implicated in procedural learning and memory, areas also implicated in OCD. In the Rauch et al. (1997) study, participants inhaled Oxygen-15 labeled CO_2 with the full paradigm lasting 32 minutes with blocks of scanning, baseline (random sequences) and implicit (recurring sequences) blocks during this time period.

The activation patterns of those with OCD was then compared to the patterns displayed by controls. Both the OCD group and the controls had comparable sequence learning. From the perspective of unaware phenomena, it is noteworthy that both OCD and controls showed no evidence of awareness of the sequence learning. The controls displayed bilateral inferior striatal activation while the OCD patients did not, instead they showed bilateral medial temporal lobe activation.

This finding is important as it may shed light on the nature of OCD and its relationship to memory as the medial temporal lobes are thought to comprise a part of the circuitry mediating explicit learning and memory. Rauch et al. (1997) interpret their data as suggesting that when neural circuitry is compromised as in the case of OCD, patients adapt by recruiting explicit learning and memory systems.

Overview of Magnetoencephalography

Magnetoencephalography (MEG) measures the magnetic fields produced by your brain. Your brain produces magnetic fields as a byproduct of electrical activity (Maxwell's Equations). MEG effectively is the magnetic equivalent of the EEG. Like the EEG, MEG measures activity in the top few centimeters of neuronal activity because of attenuation of signal strength with greater depth. Also like the EEG, it is the activity of the dendrites, specifically the postsynaptic currents that produces the electrical and magnetic fields (Hari, 1990). So, both the EEG and MEG provide a picture of dendritic functioning. The most easily quantifiable neurons by MEG are the pyramidal cells because of their orientation to the skull. Pyramidal neurons are found throughout the cortex, especially in layers III and V, and in the hippocampus and amygdala.

These neurons are the most ubiquitous excitatory neurons in the prefrontal cortex. Unlike the EEG however, the magnetic field generated by the cortical neurons is not affected by tissues (meninges and skull) above the cortex (Okada et al., 1999). MEG is also advantageous over EEG as it is able to precisely localize the source of the signal in three-dimensional space. Although MEG has been around since the late 1960s, it was not until the advent of whole scalp MEG in the 1990s that MEG became a genuine neuroimaging technique (Hari & Samelin, 2012).

How Does MEG Work?

As neurons process information they create ionic movement which causes electrical changes with respect to the inside relative to the outside of the neuron which in turn generates a weak magnetic field (Maxwell's equations). These fields are produced any time the neuron is electrically active. The strength of the magnetic field produced by thousands of neurons working simultaneously although measurable is very weak; it is estimated that at least 50,000 to 100,000 neurons must be activated simultaneously to produce a detectable magnetic field (Reite & Zimmerman, 1978; Hari, 1990).

Because the generated magnetic field is so weak, on the order of 1–10 fT (femtotesla: femto 10^{-15}, and tesla unit of magnetic induction; first measured in the CNS by Cohen, 1968) compared to ambient magnetic fields that typically surround us in the modern world at 10^8 or .1 µtesla, any MEG recordings of necessity must be taken in a heavily shielded enclosure. The first successful cortical MEG signals were demonstrated by Cohen (1968) measuring posterior alpha activity in conjunction with the electrical alpha signal.

The other key breakthrough occurred in 1962 by Josephson who laid out the principle of superconducting tunneling allowing for the development of SQUIDs (Superconducting Quantum Interference devices) (Silver & Zimmerman, 1965) which allowed for the measuring of the magnetic field without the electric reference (Cohen, 1972). The array of SQUIDs (typically 300) must be housed within an extremely cold environment using liquid helium cooled to 4K (-269° C). The millisecond timing resolution allows MEG to investigate in real time, sensory processing. For an early but thorough review of magnetic phenomena related to the central nervous system, see Reite and Zimmerman (1978).

The early single channel MEG took days to collect sufficient data to research sensory information processing compared to the current multi-channel helmet systems that can collect this information in minutes. The progress of MEG has been relatively slow compared to advances with fMRI, in part due to the greater user intervention required for data analysis with MEG (Hari & Salmelin, 2012). There are several methods of analysis and interpretation models used with MEG data.

The issue faced by those using MEG is to model the source of the fields measured externally but originating internally from electrical events. That is, localizing the source both in terms of location and timing. The simplest, most transparent, and powerful source modeling is Equivalent Current Dipole (ECD) (Hari & Salmelin, 2012). The dipole parameters (i.e., location, direction, and strength as a function of time) can be solved from the MEG patterns and related to the anatomy from MRIs. The single and multiple dipole models assume a single or a limited number of sources and then try to best model the data based on this assumption. Distributed dipole models assume activity is everywhere and seek to characterize the distribution of activity all over the brain.

Another common approach is known as beamforming; it is a forward modeling technique. In beamforming, there is no assumption about where the activity is but there is an assumption that the time courses of different sources are uncorrelated. Because estimates are of the activity overall, research using beamforming analysis tends to emphasize control conditions in their design parameters.

How Does MEG Provide Insight into Unaware Phenomena?

Much of the early research using MEG technology focused on basic sensory and motor processing (Hari & Samelin, 2012). More recently, language, visual and auditory processing have generated a significant amount of research (Hari & Samelin, 2012). There have been several recent studies investigating mirroring effects between individuals. A hallmark diagnostic characteristic of Autism Spectrum Disorder (ASD) is a deficit in social functioning. Nishitani, Avikainen, and Hari (2004) investigated mirror neuron systems in high-functioning individuals with ASD and controls by presenting images of lip forms and viewing subsequent activation patterns.

The mirror neuron system is thought to be important in imitation and understanding other peoples' intention. Nishitani et al. (2004) found early stages of processing between the ASD and control groups were similar, but there was a delay in processing in the inferior frontal regions and activation in the inferior frontal and primary motor regions were less robust as compared to controls. The pattern differences were seen bilaterally but were more pronounced in the right hemisphere.

Implicit social cognitive processing has been found to be atypical in individuals with ASD (e.g., Callenmark, Kjellin, Rönnqvist, & Bölte, 2013). One avenue that has been explored is the implicit processing of emotional faces by individuals with ASD. Implicit processing of facial emotional expressions is believed to occur rapidly and automatically and not be subject to variations in learning strategies that underlie explicit processing. Processing of emotional faces has been shown to involve bilaterally posterior and temporal (inferior and superior gyri) cortices as well as the amygdala (e.g., Bernstein & Yovel, 2015). Kovarski et al. (2019) explored the early visual processing of emotional faces (angry, happy, or neutral) in adult ASD by presenting a series of images with faces on one side of a fixation point and a scrambled pattern on the other.

Participants' task was to determine on which side of the screen the face was presented, hence the processing of the emotional content of the face was not a factor in the task performance. Both MEG and MRI data were gathered. As expected, based on previous research, the ASD group had hypoactivation in the right fusiform gyrus but in addition to this the ASD group also had early enhanced activity within the occipital regions (Kovarskie et al., 2019). One of the main advantages of MEG compared to fMRI is the fact that researchers can examine the timeline associated with cognitive processing. For example, in the Kovarskie et al. study, they were able to determine that the hypoactivation of the fusiform gyrus occurred at 150ms post exposure.

Functional magnetic resonance imaging (fMRI)

Functional magnetic resonance imaging or functional MRI (fMRI) provides a measure of brain activity by detecting changes in cerebral blood flow associated with commensurate changes in neuronal activity. Thus, when an area of the brain is engaged, blood flow to that region also increases. fMRI has been used to explore brain regions and local networks, as well as providing insight into brain organization and functional communication within brain networks (Van den Heuvel & Pol, 2010).

fMRI and Racial Bias

As described in chapter 13 and while it may not be a familiar concept to some, the world of unaware phenomena may also include bias among its many inhabitants. Interestingly, fMRI has been used as a tool to uncover racial bias and it has been reported that racial bias predicted activity in right dorsolateral prefrontal cortex (DLPFC) and that this region also predicted interference on the Stroop Color-Naming Task after interracial contact (Richeson et al. 2003). In other words, functional imaging was able to identify areas of the brain that showed differential levels of activation as a result of presumed racial bias expressed as executive processing interference as a function of interracial interactions. Richeson (2003) reported that activity in the right dorsolateral prefrontal cortex, which is implicated in executive control, was also associated with the expression of racial bias and its impact on executive control in response to black faces.

Further expanding on this, after white participants completed an unobtrusive measure of racial bias they interacted with a black individual, and then completed an unrelated Stroop Color Naming test. Activity in the DLPFC region predicted Stroop interference after the interracial interaction, and that it statistically mediated the relation between racial bias and Stroop interference. This interference was interpreted as reflecting a depletion in resources due to temporary executive dysfunction observed in racially biased individuals following interracial contact. Patterns of brain activation occurred outside of the participants' awareness, providing a window through which the inner workings of the brain could be imaged in response to interracial interaction.

Taken together, these imaging techniques provide insights into both the spatial and temporal characteristic of processes that can occur within the central nervous system in the absence of awareness. They also provide insight into how we respond to other human beings in ways beyond our conscious awareness.

Conclusion

Before reading this book, you might have asked why does all of this matter and what is its significance or how meaningful are unaware phenomena in our daily lives. At this point, you have hopefully become convinced that the importance and meaning resides in the fact that so many of our memories, perceptions, tastes, preferences, biases, and beliefs are expressed on an unaware, largely non-conscious level.

In other words, it appears as if our lives and actions are guided and influenced by factors about which we may know very little but, nevertheless, these factors can alter the quality, substance and trajectory of our lives . . . our loves, our likes and our dislikes.

While not without controversy, the preponderance of evidence emerging from the scientific literature supports the idea that there are windows through which we can see into the abyss of this unawareness, past the darkness. In fact, there is ample evidence demonstrating that we are capable of reacting to faces and places in distinct ways although we may profess to have never seen or visited these faces or places. Yet our responses, whether they are manifested as more fluent processing, preference or changes in physiology suggest that we have seen these faces and occupied these places in one mode or another.

Simply put, there are multiple means, modalities and mechanisms that point in the same direction. That is, previously seen or experienced information can alter our behavior in ways beyond our awareness and are expressed and manifested in a variety of contexts. For example, through faster response times, differentiated physiological profiles within the autonomic and central nervous system, changes in perceptual-motor responses, faster and more fluent processing, preferences for or perhaps faster re-learning of information that was previously learned, although no longer consciously remembered.

But what does it all mean on a pragmatic level? These findings may have implications for both the speed and nature of our decision-making, the choices we make in life and the friends we choose. It may have implications for the notion of free will. In other words, do we truly know why we do what we do, feel what we feel, know what we know, or prefer one painting or song over another?

In order to better understand all of these processes, one would need to probe further into the world of unawareness to untangle the many factors that have become interwoven in a complex fabric created over the course of many years and life experiences. Experiences, memories, emotions and physiological and neurological response patterns have been integrated into a vast number of arrays that can be reactivated in response to elements embedded in these arrays by virtue of their association qualitatively, temporally or spatially.

The path forward may require that we step backward, in order to understand who we are, how we got to be that way and where we are headed. For those individuals whose memories may have become faint or appear to have been lost forever; or have compromised vision and cognitive skills; or lost their sense of continuity and self; left only with a vague or non-existent sense of familiarity for places and faces, there may be integral parts of their lives that can be reached via new and novel pathways to self-discovery.

Pathways that provide a way to access areas that may appear to be isolated and removed from their phenomenological awareness. Pathways that may provide insight into the theoretical underpinnings of complex memory, cognitive and perceptual-sensory functions. Pathways that may provide a route to help facilitate recovery and remediation of the seemingly lost or inaccessible using creative modes of discovery and re-discovery.

If previously unreachable memories for faces, places, skills, or knowledge can be accessed, we may be able to help many who have suffered from neurologic, neurodevelopmental and neuropsychiatric disorders begin the process of recovery. Shattered pieces of life and self that while isolated, and only weakly connected to conscious experience, can be re-invoked, re-invigorated and reincarnated in ways that reintegrate the self.

The implications of the world of unaware phenomena are profound. Our ability to reach the unknown realms within has implications for multiple domains: education, career, activities of daily living, interpersonal relationships, learning, and social cognition. If we can recover or identify information that was thought to be lost or about which we were unaware, our lives can become richer, fuller and more functional.

Certain types of learning involving procedural memory can be recovered and in some instances re-encoded so that individuals with neurologic injuries can learn and re-learn career-related skills and knowledge. Information and learning may be embedded in the deepest recesses of the mind and while individuals may not explicitly recall learning episodes or contexts, they can still demonstrate and apply the skills and knowledge they have learned.

These unaware memories can influence so many aspects of our lives and culture and, in fact, may have been the inspiration for art and poetry—and perhaps also bias and discrimination. One might wonder what portion of our lives is influenced by information, associations and factors beyond our awareness. Do we make conscious, willful, aware decisions or do we act and think in ways that are controlled or influenced by factors about which we are unaware?

Taken together, this world of unaware phenomena may be expressed in so many ways, using multiple methodologies and techniques including behavioral and priming paradigms, implicit measurement, procedural memory, autonomic nervous system correlates, functional imaging, EEG/ERP and computer-based measures, all of which can be expressed across the developmental spectrum.

This unaware world provides insights into lost memories, loves, likes, preferences, biases, learning, trauma, language, visual processing, faces, places, neurologic disorders, unawareness of deficits, confabulation, anxiety, and computer skill learning, among others. What is striking is how pervasive this world is. How it is a part of so many aspects of our everyday lives and how impactful it can be. And what is most remarkable is how we are largely unaware of the factors that guide our behaviors, reactions, and processing of our internal and external world. Who we are and why we do what we do is to a great extent an enigma. The greatest mystery may not be the image in the mirror, but how this inner world is reflected in our everyday lives, in ways unknown to our conscious awareness, but in ways that exert concrete and palpable effects on who we are and how we respond to the world and, perhaps, how the world responds to us.

Where does this journey lead? What's next? How do we use these insights? What are the practical implications? For one thing, this journey may lead to more effective rehabilitation of impairments in memory. We can build on these insights and develop more sensitive assessment tools that can tap into memories that are not normally accessible and we can establish what time periods and types of memory may be compromised or inaccessible.

Therapists may be able to probe a client's memory, emotions and attitudes in ways that are not feasible using standard techniques. The information that is gleaned by using these indirect techniques may help illuminate what has been hidden and inaccessible for much of a person's life.

Using these tools for self-exploration, clients may achieve new insights about themselves and their lives as well as the factors and forces that have shaped who they are. Perhaps too, this inner world may provide directions and pathways that can lead to meaningful change, the identification of psychological obstacles and perhaps foster enhanced well-being.

The inner world of unaware phenomena may also have applicability to the area of forensics. For example, we may be able to reach long-forgotten or suppressed memories; memories of crimes, perpetrators or witnesses. The information derived and the methodology used to retrieve it may prove valuable in investigations of all types ranging from civilian crime to military investigations.

The inner world may also help us reconstruct the life of an accident victim with amnesia. That is, we may be able to retrieve and reassemble disparate parts of a person's life, weaving together a person's history, likes and loves. We may be able to assemble and re-integrate the images, events, learning and melodies from a person's life history. Moreover, we may be able to rehabilitate an individual's career and work-related knowledge and skills, in essence, reintegrate an individual into their own unique life history.

Individuals who have suffered neurologic injury associated with disease, trauma or various syndromes and disorders and whose careers and education have been interrupted and compromised may be able to be retrained. That is, while skills and knowledge may be consciously inaccessible, they can nevertheless be used as scaffolding for rebuilding, relearning and applying that knowledge and those skills to novel situations and contexts. New learning can be built on old learning, in ways that don't require recall of the original learning episode(s).

As we gain greater access to and awareness of this world within, we may achieve a greater understanding of who we are and how and why we react to the world the way we do. We will gain new and sensitive tools for illuminating long-forgotten events, reveal likes and dislikes, biases and prejudice, predilections toward movies, melodies, foods and fantasies, political candidates and poetry, and build on existing learning, oftentimes in the absence of awareness, but in ways that make future learning more efficient.

But more than anything else, this pathway is a road that may lead to self-discovery and a way and means to achieve self-illumination and the realization that we do not have to be cut off from places and spaces that were thought to be either inaccessible or, in fact, unknown. And while not a panacea, as some information and memories will be lost forever, it may still provide a reflection that mirrors who we have been, where we have traveled and who we may become.

References

Addante, R. J. (2015). A Critical Role of the Human Hippocampus in an Electrophysiological Measure of Implicit Memory, *NeuroImage,* 109, 515–528. doi.org/10.1016/j.neuroimage.2014.12.069.

Ahr, E., Houdé, O., and Borst, G. (2016). Inhibition of the Mirror Generalization Process in Reading in School-Aged Children. *Journal of Experimental Child Psychology*, *145*, 157–165. doi.org/10.1016/j.jecp.2015.12.009.

Alajouanine, T. (1956). Verbal Realization in Aphasia. *Brain*, *79*(1), 1–28.

American Psychiatric Association. (2013). *Diagnostic and Statistical Manual of Mental Disorders*, 5th edition. Arlington, VA: Author. doi.org/10.1176/appi. books.9780890425596.

Amir, N., McNally, R. J., and Wiegartz, P. S. (1996). Implicit Memory Bias for Threat in Posttraumatic Stress Disorder. *Cognitive Therapy and Research*, *20*(6), 625–635.

Amodio, D. M., Harmon-Jones, E., Devine, P. G., Curtin, J. J., Hartley, S. L., and Covert, A. E. (2004). Neural Signals for the Detection of Unintentional Race Bias. *Psychological Science*, *15*(2), 88–93.

Angwin, A., Chenery, H., Copland, D., Murdoch, B., and Silburn, P. (2005). Summation of Semantic Priming and Complex Sentence Comprehension in Parkinson's Disease. *Brain Research. Cognitive Brain Research*, *25*(1), 78–89. doi. org/10.1016/j.cogbrainres.2005.04.008.

Angwin, A., Chenery, H., Copland, D., Murdoch, B., and Silburn, P. (2007). The Speed of Lexical Activation Is Altered in Parkinson's Disease. *Journal of Clinical and Experimental Neuropsychology*, *29*(1), 73–85. doi. org/10.1080/13803390500507188.

Annett, M. (1991) Reading Upside Down and Mirror Text in Groups Differing for Right Minus Left Hand Skill, *European Journal of Cognitive Psychology*, 3:4, 363–377. doi.org/10.1080/09541449108406234.

Arnott, W., Chenery, H., Murdoch, B., and Silburn, P. (2001). Semantic Priming in Parkinsons Disease: Evidence for Delayed Spreading Activation. *Journal of Clinical and Experimental Neuropsychology*, *23*(4), 502–519. doi.org/10.1076/jcen.23.4.502.1224.

Azzopardi, P., and Cowey, A. (1997). Is Blindsight Like Normal, Near-Threshold Vision? *Proceedings of the National Academy of Sciences*, *94*(25), 14190–14194.

Baddeley, A. D. (1982). Implications of Neuropsychological Evidence for Theories of Normal Memory. *Philosophical Transactions of the Royal Society of London. B, Biological Sciences*, *298*(1089), 59–57

Barr, R., Vieira, A., and Rovee-Collier, C. (2002). Bidirectional Priming in Infants. *Memory & Cognition, 30*(2), 246–255. dx.doi.org/10.3758/BF03195285.

Barrett, L. F. (1998). Discrete Emotions or Dimensions? The Role of Valence Focus and Arousal Focus, Cognition and Emotion, 12:4, 579–599, DOI: 10.1080/026999398379574.

Barrett, L. F. (2004). Feelings or Words? Understanding the Content in Self-Report Ratings of Experienced Emotion. *Journal of Personality and Social Psychology*, 87, 266–281.

Barrett, L. F. (2017). The Theory of Constructed Emotion: An Active Inference Account of Interoception and Categorization. *Social Cognitive and Affective Neuroscience*, *12*(1), 1–23.

Barrett, L. F., Tugade, M. M., and Engle, R. W. (2004). Individual Differences in Working Memory Capacity and Dual-Process Theories of the Mind. Psychological Bulletin, 130(4), 553–573. doi.org/10.1037/0033-2909.130.4.553.

Batterink, L., Reber, P., Neville, H., and Paller, K. (2015). Implicit and Explicit Contributions to Statistical Learning. *Journal of Memory and Language*, 83, 62–78. doi.org/10.1016/j.jml.2015.04.004.

Bauer, R. M. (1984). Autonomic Recognition of Names and Faces in Prosopagnosia: A Neuropsychological Application of the Guilty Knowledge Test. *Neuropsychologia*, *22*(4), 457–469.

Bauer, R. M. (1986). The Cognitive Psychophysiology of Prosopagnosia. In *Aspects of Face Processing,* 253–267. Springer, Dordrecht.

Bechara, A., Tranel, D., Damasio, H., Adolphs, R., Rockland, C., Damasio, A. R. (1995). Double Dissociation of Conditioning and Declarative Knowledge Relative to the Amygdala and Hippocampus in Humans. *Science*. Aug 25; 269(5227): 1115–1118. doi: 10.1126/science.7652558. PMID: 7652558.

Ben-Shakhar, G. (1994). The Roles of Stimulus Novelty and Significance in Determining the Electrodermal Orienting Response: Interactive versus Additive Approaches. *Psychophysiology*, *31*(4), 402–411.

Benson, D. F., Djenderedjian, A., Miller, B. L., Pachana, N. A., Chang, L., Itti, L., and Mena, I. (1996). Neural Basis of Confabulation. *Neurology*, *46*(5), 1239–1239.

Bentin, S., and Moscovitch, M. (1990). Psychophysiological Indices of Implicit Memory Performance. *Bulletin of the Psychonomic Society, 28*(4), 346–352. dx.doi.org/10.3758/BF03334040.

Bernstein, M. and Yovel, G. (2015). Two Neural Pathways of Face Processing: A Critical Evaluation of Current Models. Neuroscience & Biobehavioral Reviews *55*, 536–546. doi.org/10.1016/j.neubiorev.2015.06.010.

Besson, G., Ceccaldi, M., Tramoni, E., Felician, O., Didic, M., and Barbeau, E. (2015). Fast, but Not Slow, Familiarity Is Preserved in Patients with Amnestic Mild Cognitive Impairment. *Cortex*, *65*, 36–49. doi.org/10.1016/j.cortex.2014.10.020.

Blanton, H., and Jaccard, J. (2006). Arbitrary Metrics in Psychology. *American Psychologist, 61*(1), 27–41. dx.doi.org/10.1037/0003-066X.61.1.27.

Blanton, H., and Jaccard, J. (2006). Tests of Multiplicative Models in Psychology: A Case Study Using the Unified Theory of Implicit Attitudes, Stereotypes, Self-Esteem, and Self-Concept. *Psychological Review, 113*(1), 155–166. dx.doi. org/10.1037/0033-295X.113.1.155.

Boldt, A., Stürmer, B., Gaschler, R., Schacht, A., and Sommer, W. (2013). Get Out of Here, Quick! Problems with Transparent Labels on Glass Doors. *Journal of Experimental Psychology: Applied, 19*(3), 241–253. doi.org/10.1037/a0034079.

Bondi, M. W., and Kaszniak, A.W. (1991). Implicit and Explicit Memory in Alzheimer's Disease and Parkinson's Disease. *Journal of Clinical and Experimental Neuropsychology*, 339–358. doi.org/10.1080/01688639108401048.

Boucsein, W. (1992). Electrodermal Indices of Emotion and Stress, chapter 3. *Electrodermal Activity*, 369–391.

Bowers, J. S., and Marsolek, C. J. (2003). *Rethinking Implicit Memory*. Oxford University Press.

Bowler, J. L., Bowler, M. C., and James, L. R. (2011). The Cognitive Underpinnings of Addiction, *Substance Use & Misuse, 46*(8), 1060–1071, DOI: 10.3109/10826084.2011.552934.

Bradley, M. M., Cuthbert, B. N., & Lang, P. J. (1990). "Startle Reflex Modification: Emotion or Attention?" *Psychophysiology, 27*(5), 513–522.

Brainerd, C. J., Nakamura, K., and Lee, W.-F. A. (2019). Recollection Is Fast and Slow. *Journal of Experimental Psychology: Learning, Memory, and Cognition, 45*(2), 302–319. doi.org/10.1037/xlm0000588.

Breen, E., Pomper, R., and Saffran, J. (2019). Phonological Learning Influences Label–Object Mapping in Toddlers. *Journal of Speech, Language, and Hearing Research, 62*(6), 1923–1932. doi.org/10.1044/2019_jslhr-l-18-0131.

Bruce, V., and Young, A. (1986). Understanding Face Recognition. *British Journal of Psychology, 77*(3), 305–327.

Bruyer, R., Laterre, C., Seron, X., Feyereisen, P., Strypstein, E., Pierrard, E., and Rectem, D. (1983). A Case of Prosopagnosia with Some Preserved Covert Remembrance of Familiar Faces. *Brain and Cognition, 2*(3), 257–284.

Bryant, R. A., Creamer, M., O'Donnell, M., Silove, D., and McFarlane, A. C. (2008). A Multisite Study of Initial Respiration Rate and Heart Rate as Predictors of Posttraumatic Stress Disorder. *The Journal of Clinical Psychiatry, 69*(11), 1694–1701.

Buckner, R. L., Peterson, S. E., Ojemann, J. G., Miezin, F. M., Squire, L. R., and Raichle, M. E. (1995). Functional Anatomical Studies of Explicit and Implicit Memory Retrieval Tasks. *The Journal of Neuroscience.* 15(1) 12–29. doi. org/10.1523/JNEUROSCI.15-01-00012.1995.

Burgund, E., Marsolek, C., and Luciana, M. (2003). Serotonin Levels Influence Patterns of Repetition Priming. *Neuropsychology, 17*(1), 161–170. doi. org/10.1037/0894-4105.17.1.161.

Burling, R., Armstrong, D. F., Blount, B. G., Callaghan, Catherine, A. Foster, M. L., King, B. J., Parker, S. T., Sakura, O., Stokoe, W. C., Wallace, R., Wallman, J., Whiten, A., Wilcox, S., and Wynn, T. (1993). Primate Calls, Human Language, and Nonverbal Communication [and Comments and Reply]. *Current Anthropology, 34*(1), 25–53. doi.org/10.1086/204132.

Burton, A. M., Young, A. W., Bruce, V., Johnston, R. A., and Ellis, A. W. (1991). Understanding Covert Recognition. *Cognition, 39*(2), 129–166.

Callenmark, B., Kjellin, L., Rönnqvist, L., and Bölte, S. (2013). Explicit versus Implicit Social Cognition Testing in Autism Spectrum Disorder. *Autism: The International Journal of Research and Practice, 18*(6), 684–693. doi. org/10.1177/1362361313492393.

Carlesimo, G. A. (1994). Perceptual and Conceptual Priming in Amnesic and Alcoholic Patients. *Neuropsychologia 32*, 903–921. doi.org/10.1016/0028-3932(94)90042-6.

Carlesimo, G., Marfia, G., Loasses, A., and Caltagirone, C. (1996). Perceptual and Conceptual Components in Implicit and Explicit Stem Completion. *Neuropsychol ogia, 34*(8), 785–792. doi.org/10.1016/0028-3932(95)00162-X.

Carlesimo, G., Mauri, M., Fadda, L., Turriziani, P., and Caltagirone, C. (2001). Intact Cross-Modality Text-Specific Repetition Priming in Patients with Alzheimer's Disease. *Journal of Clinical and Experimental Neuropsychology, 23*(5), 569–580. doi.org/10.1076/jcen.23.5.569.1244.

Cermak, L.S. and Stiassny, D. (1982). Recall Failure Following Successful Generation and Recognition of Responses by Alcoholic Korsakoff Patients, *Brain and Cognition, 1*(2), 165–176, doi.org/10.1016/0278-2626(82)90014-8.

Cermak, L. S., Talbot, N., Chandler, K., and Wolbarst, L. R. (1985). The Perceptual Priming Phenomenon in Amnesia. *Neuropsychologia, 23*(5), 615–622. dx.doi. org/10.1016/0028-3932(85)90063-6.

Cherry, S. R., Badawi, R. D., Karp, J. S., Moses, W. W., Price, P., and Jones, T. (2017). Total-Body Imaging: Transforming the Role of Positron Emission Tomography. *Science Translational Medicine, 9*(381), eaaf6169. doi.org/10.1126/scitranslmed.aaf6169.

Chiu, P., Ambady, N., and Deldin, P. (2004). Contingent Negative Variation to Emotional In- and Out-Group Stimuli Differentiates High- and Low-Prejudiced Individuals. *Journal of Cognitive Neuroscience, 16*(10), 1830–1839.

Chng, K., Chng, K., Yap, M., Yap, M., Goh, W., and Goh, W. (2019). Cross-Modal Masked Repetition and Semantic Priming in Auditory Lexical Decision. *Psychonomic Bulletin & Review, 26*(2), 599–608. doi.org/10.3758/s13423-018-1540-8.

Christiansen, M. (2019). Implicit Statistical Learning: A Tale of Two Literatures. *Topics in Cognitive Science, 11*(3), 468–481. doi.org/10.1111/tops.12332.

Cocchini, G., Beschin, N. and Della Sala, S. (2002). Chronic Anosognosia: A Case Report and Theoretical Account. *Neuropsychologia, 40*, 2030–2038.

Cohen, D. (1968). Magnetoencephalography: Evidence of Magnetic Fields Produced by Alpha Currents. *Science 161*, 3843, 784–786. doi.org/10.1126/science.161.3843.784.

Cohen, N. J. (1984). Preserved Learning Capacity in Amnesia: Evidence for Multiple Memory Systems. In *Neuropsychology of memory*, Edited by Squire, L. R. and Butters, N. New York: Guilford.

Cohen, D. (1972). Magnetoencephalography: Detection of the Brain's Electrical Activity with a Superconducting Magnetometer. *Science 175*, 4022, 664–666. doi. org/10.1126/science.175.4022.664.

Cohen, N., and Squire, L. (1980). Preserved Learning and Retention of Pattern-Analyzing Skill in Amnesia: Dissociation of Knowing How and Knowing That. *Science (American Association for the Advancement of Science)*, *210*(4466), 207–210. doi.org/10.1126/science.7414331.

Conway, C. M., and Christiansen, M. H. (2005). Modality-Constrained Statistical Learning of Tactile, Visual, and Auditory Sequences. *Journal of Experimental Psychology: Learning, Memory, and Cognition*, *31*(1), 24.

Conway, C., and Pisoni, D. (2008). Neurocognitive Basis of Implicit Learning of Sequential Structure and Its Relation to Language Processing. *Annals of the New York Academy of Sciences*, *1145*(1), 113–131. doi.org/10.1196/annals.1416.009.

Correll, J., Park, B., Judd, C. M., and Wittenbrink, B. (2007). The Influence of Stereotypes on Decisions to Shoot. *European Journal of Social Psychology*, *37*(6), 1102–1117.

Corteen, R. S., and Wood, B. (1972). Autonomic Responses to Shock-Associated Words in an Unattended Channel. *Journal of Experimental Psychology*, *94*(3), 308–313. dx.doi.org/10.1037/h0032759.

Cowey, A. (2010). The Blindsight Saga. *Experimental brain research*, *200*(1), 3–24.

Craik, F. I. M., Rose, N. S., and Gopie, N. (2015). Recognition Without Awareness: Encoding and Retrieval Factors. *Journal of Experimental Psychology: Learning, Memory, and Cognition*, 41(5), 1271–1281. doi.org/10.1037/xlm0000137.

Critchley, M. (1953). *The Parietal Lobes*. Williams and Wilkins, Oxford.

Crovitz, H. E, Harvey, M. T., and McClanahan, S. (1979). Hidden Memory: A Rapid Method for the Study of Amnesia Using Perceptual Learning. *Cortex, 17*, 273–278.

Cunningham, W. A., Johnson, M. K., Raye, C. L., Gatenby, J. C., Gore, J. C., and Banaji, M. R. (2004). Separable Neural Components in the Processing of Black and White faces. *Psychological science*, *15*(12), 806–813.

Curran, T., DeBuse, C., Woroch, B., and Hirshman, E. (2006). Combined Pharmacological and Electrophysiological Dissociation of Familiarity and Recollection. *Journal of Neuroscience*, *26*(7), 1979–1985.

Dalla Barba, G., Boissé, M. F., Bartolomeo, P., and Bachoud-Lévi, A. C. (1997). Confabulation Following Rupture of Posterior Communicating Artery. *Cortex*, *33*(3), 563–570.

Damasio, A. R. (1985). Prosopagnosia. *Trends in Neurosciences*, *8*, 132–135.

Damasio, H. (1995). *Human Brain Anatomy in Computerized Images*. Oxford University Press.

Daum, I., Channon, S., and Canavan, A. G. (1989). Classical Conditioning in Patients with Severe Memory Problems. *Journal of Neurology, Neurosurgery and Psychiatry*, *52*(1), 47–51.

Defrise, M., Kinahan, P. E., and Michel, C. (2003). Image Reconstruction Algorithms in PET. In *Positron Emission Tomography: Basic Science and Clinical Practice*, 91–114. New York: Springer-Verlag. DOI: 10.1007/1-84628-007-9_4.

de Haan, E. H. F., Young, A., & Newcombe, F. (1987). Face Recognition without Awareness. *Cognitive Neuropsychology*, *4*(4), 385–415.

de Haan, E. H. F., Young, A. W., Newcombe, F. (1991). Covert and Overt Recognition in Prosopagnosia, Brain, *114*(6), 2575–2591, doi.org/10.1093/brain/114.6.2575.

DeLuca, J. (1993). Predicting Neurobehavioral Patterns Following Anterior Communicating Artery Aneurysm. *Cortex, 29,* 639–647.

DeLuca, J. (2000). A Cognitive Neuroscience Perspective on Confabulation. *Neuropsychoanalysis, 2*(2), 119–132.

DeLuca, J. and Cicerone, K. D. (1991). Confabulation Following Aneurysm of the Anterior Communicating Artery. *Cortex, 27,* 417–423

DeLuca, J., and Diamond, B. J. (1995). Aneurysm of the Anterior Communicating Artery: A Review of Neuroanatomical and Neuropsychological Sequelae. *Journal of Clinical and Experimental Neuropsychology, 17*(1), 100–121.

De Renzi, E. (1986). Prosopagnosia in Two Patients with CT Scan Evidence of Damage Confined to the Right Hemisphere. *Neuropsychologia, 24*(3), 385–389.

De Renzi, E., Faglioni, P., Grossi, D., and Nichelli, P. (1991). Apperceptive and Associative Forms of Prosopagnosia. *Cortex, 27*(2), 213–221.

de Wit, B., and Kinoshita, S. (2015). The Masked Semantic Priming Effect Is Task Dependent: Reconsidering the Automatic Spreading Activation Process. *Journal of Experimental Psychology. Learning, Memory, and Cognition, 41*(4), 1062–1075. doi.org/10.1037/xlm0000074

Diamond, B., DeLuca, J. and Richards, J. (2003). Physiological Discrimination of Confabulations from Realities in ACoA Aneurysm. *Journal of the International Neuropsychological Society (JINS),* 9 (2), 151, INS, Hawaii.

Diamond B. J., Haines, E. L., Moors A. C., Mosley, J. E., McKim D., Moreines, J. (2012). Implicit Bias, Executive Control and Information Processing Speed. *Journal of Cognition and Culture 12,* 183–193.

Diamond, B. J., Mayes, A. R., Meudell, P. R. (1996). Autonomic and Recognition Indices of Memory in Amnesic and Healthy Control Subjects. *Cortex, 32*(3), 439–459. doi.org/10.1016/S0010-9452(96)80003-7.

Diamond, B. J., Mayes, A. R., and Meudell, P. R. (2011). Priming, Recognition and Autonomic Discrimination in Amnesia. *Neurocase, 17*(1), 76–90.

Diamond, B. J., Valentine, T., Mayes, A. R., Sandel, M. E. (1994) Evidence of Covert Recognition in a Prosopagnosic Patient. *Cortex, 30,* 377–393.

Dirnberger, G., and Novak-Knollmueller, J. (2013). Motor and Perceptual Sequence Learning: Different Time Course of Parallel Processes. *NeuroReport: For Rapid Communication of Neuroscience Research, 24*(10), 578 –583. doi.org/10.1097/WNR.0b013e3283625cfa.

Dirnberger, G., Novak, J., and Nasel, C. (2013). Perceptual Sequence Learning Is More Severely Impaired than Motor Sequence Learning in Patients with Chronic Cerebellar Stroke. *Journal of Cognitive Neuroscience, 25*(12), 2207–2215. doi.org/10.1162/jocn_a_00444.

Dobbins, I., Schnyer, D., Verfaellie, M., and Schacter, D. (2004). Cortical Activity Reductions during Repetition Priming Can Result from Rapid Response Learning. *Nature* (London), *428*(6980), 316–319. doi.org/10.1038/nature02400.

Dovidio, J. F., Kawakami, K., and Gaertner, S. L. (2002). Implicit and Explicit Prejudice and Interracial Interaction. *Journal of Personality and Social Psychology.* 82: 62–68.

Doyen, S., Klein, O., Simons, D., and Cleeremans, A. (2014). On the Other Side of the Mirror: Priming in Cognitive and Social Psychology. *Social Cognition*, 32(Supplement), 12–32. doi.org/10.1521/soco.2014.32.supp.12.

Drummey, A. B., and Newcombe, N. (1995). Remembering versus Knowing the Past: Children's Explicit and Implicit Memories for Pictures. *Journal of Experimental Child Psychology*, 59(3), 549–565. doi.org/10.1006/jecp.1995.1025.

Erickson, L., and Thiessen, E. (2015). Statistical Learning of Language: Theory, Validity, and Predictions of a Statistical Learning Account of Language Acquisition. *Developmental Review*, 37, 66–108. doi.org/10.1016/j.dr.2015.05.002.

Erskine, R. G. (2008). Psychotherapy of Unconscious Experience. *Transactional Analysis Journal, 38*(2), 128–138. dx.doi.org/10.1177/036215370803800206.

Feldman, J., Kerr, B., and Streissguth, A. (1995). Correlational Analyses of Procedural and Declarative Learning Performance. *Intelligence (Norwood), 20*(1), 87–114. doi.org/10.1016/0160-2896(95)90007-1.

Ferbinteanu, J. (2019). Memory Systems 2018: Towards a New Paradigm. *Neurobiology of Learning and Memory, 157*, 61–78. doi.org/10.1016/j.nlm.2018.11.005.

Fendrich, R., Wessinger, C. M., and Gazzaniga, M. S. (2001). Speculations on the Neural Basis of Islands of Blindsight. *Progress in Brain Research, 134*, 353–366.

Field, M., Wiers, R. W., Christiansen, P., Fillmore, M. T., and Verster, J. C. (2010). Acute Alcohol Effects on Inhibitory Control and Implicit Cognition: Implications for Loss of Control over Drinking. *Alcoholism, Clinical and Experimental Research, 34*(8), 1346–1352. doi.org/10.1111/j.1530-0277.2010. 01218.x.

Filoteo, J., Friedrich, F., Rilling, L., Davis, J., Stricker, J., and Prenovitz, M. (2003). Semantic and Cross-Case Identity Priming in Patients with Parkinson's Disease. *Journal of Clinical and Experimental Neuropsychology*, 25(4), 441–456. doi. org/10.1076/jcen.25.4.441.13874.

Fiser, J., and Aslin, R. N. (2002). Statistical Learning of Higher-Order Temporal Structure from Visual Shape Sequences. *Journal of Experimental Psychology: Learning, Memory, and Cognition*, 28(3), 458.

Fiser, J., and Aslin, R. N. (2001). Unsupervised Statistical Learning of Higher-Order Spatial Structures from Visual Scenes. *Psychological Science*, 12(6), 499–504.

Frost, R., Armstrong, B., and Christiansen, M. (2019). Statistical Learning Research: A Critical Review and Possible New Directions. *Psychological Bulletin, 145*(12), 1128–1153. doi.org/10.1037/bul0000210.

Frost, R., Armstrong, B. C., Siegelman, N., and Christiansen, M. H. (2015). Domain Generality versus Modality Specificity: The Paradox of Statistical Learning. *Trends in Cognitive Sciences, 19*(3), 117–125. dx.doi.org/10.1016/j.tics.2014.12.010.

Frysinger, R. C., and Harper, R. M. (1989). Cardiac and Respiratory Correlations with Unit Discharge in Human Amygdala and Hippocampus. *Electroencephalography and Clinical Neurophysiology, 72*(6), 463–470.

Gebauer, G. F., and Mackintosh, N. J. (2007). Psychometric Intelligence Dissociates Implicit and Explicit Learning. *Journal of Experimental Psychology: Learning, Memory, and Cognition, 33*(1), 34–54. dx.doi.org/10.1037/0278-7393.33.1.34.

Glaser, J., and Kihlstrom, J. F. (2005). Compensatory Automaticity: Unconscious Volition Is Not an Oxymoron. *The New Unconscious*, 171–195.

Glisky, E. L., Schacter, D. L., and Tulving, E. (1986). Computer Learning by Memory-Impaired Patients: Acquisition and Retention of Complex Knowledge. *N europsychologia 24*(3), 313–328.

Gold, D., Park, N., Murphy, K., and Troyer, A. (2015). Naturalistic Action Performance Distinguishes Amnestic Mild Cognitive Impairment from Healthy Aging. *Journal of the International Neuropsychological Society*, *21*(6), 419–428. doi.org/10.1017/S135561771500048X.

Gold, P. B., Engdahl, B. E., Eberly, R. E., Blake, R. J., Page, W. F., and Frueh, B. C. (2000). Trauma Exposure, Resilience, Social Support, and PTSD Construct Validity among Former Prisoners of War. *Social Psychiatry and Psychiatric Epidemiology*, *35*(1), 36–42.

Goldin-Meadow, S. (2003). The Resilience of Language: What Gesture Creation in Deaf Children Can Tell Us About How All Children Learn Language. In *The Resilience of Language*. Abingdon-on-Thames, UK: Taylor and Francis Group.

Goodale, M., Milner, A. D, Jakobson, L. S, Carey, D. P. (1991). A Neurological Dissociation between Perceiving Objects and Grasping Them. *Nature* (London), *349*(6305), 154–156. doi.org/10.1038/349154a0.

Graf, P., Shimamura, A., and Squire, L. (1985). Priming Across Modalities and Priming Across Category Levels: Extending the Domain of Preserved Function in Amnesia. *Journal of Experimental Psychology. Learning, Memory, and Cognition*, *11*(2), 386–396. doi.org/10.1037/0278-7393.11.2.386.

Greenwald, A. G., McGhee, D. E., and Schwartz, J. L. (1998). Measuring Individual Differences in Implicit Cognition: The Implicit Association Test. *Journal of Personality and Social Psychology*, *74*(6), 1464.

Greenwald, A. G., Nosek, B. A., and Banaji, M. R. (2003). Understanding and Using the Implicit Association Test: I. An Improved Scoring Algorithm. *Journal of Personality and Social Psychology*, *85*(2), 197.

Guillery, B., Desgranges, B., Katis, S., de, l. S., Viader, F., and Eustache, F. (2001). Semantic Acquisition without Memories: Evidence from Transient Global Amnesia. *NeuroReport: For Rapid Communication of Neuroscience Research, 12*(17), 3865–3869. dx.doi.org/10.1097/00001756-200112040-00052.

Hamann, S., and Squire, L. (1997). Intact Perceptual Memory in the Absence of Conscious Memory. *Behavioral Neuroscience*, *111*(4), 850–854. doi.org/10.1037//0735-7044.111.4.850.

Hamm, A. O., and Vaitl, D. (1996). Affective Learning: Awareness and Aversion. *Ps ychophysiology*, *33*(6), 698–710.

Hannesdottir, K. and Morris, R. (2007). Primary and Secondary Anosognosia for Memory Impairment in Patients with Alzheimer's Disease. *Cortex, 43*, 1020–1030.

Hari, R. (1990). The Neuromagnetic Method in the Study of the Human Auditory Cortex. In: Grandori F., Hoke M., Romani G. L. (eds.), *Auditory Evoked Magnetic Fields and Potentials. (Advances in Audiology, 6)* Basel: Karger, 222–282.

Hari, R., and Salmelin, R. (2012). Magnetoencephalography: From SQUIDs to Neuroscience. *NeuroImage* (Orlando, FL), *61*(2), 386–396. doi.org/10.1016/j.neuroimage.2011.11.074.

Harrington D. L., Haaland K. Y., Yeo R. A., and Marder E. (1990). Procedural Memory in Parkinson's Disease: Impaired Motor but Not Visuoperceptual Learning. *Journal of Clinical Experimental Neuropsychology, 12*(2), 323–339. doi. org/10.1080/01688639008400978.

Hart, A. J., Whalen, P. J., Shin, L. M., McInerney, S. C., Fischer, H., and Rauch, S. L. (2000). Differential Response in the Human Amygdala to Racial Outgroup vs Ingroup Face Stimuli. *Neuroreport, 11*(11), 2351–2354.

Hartman, M., Knopman, D. S., and Nissen, M. J. (1989). Implicit Learning of New Verbal Associations. *Journal of Experimental Psychology: Learning, Memory, and Cognition, 15*(6), 1070–1082. doi.org/10.1037/0278-7393.15.6.1070.

Hasher, L., and Zacks, R. T. (1979). Automatic and Effortful Processes in Memory. *Journal of Experimental Psychology: General, 108*(3), 356.

Heyman, T., Van Rensbergen, B., Storms, G., Hutchison, K., and De Deyne, S. (2015). The Influence of Working Memory Load on Semantic Priming. *Journal of Experimental Psychology: Learning, Memory, and Cognition, 41*(3), 911–920. doi. org/10.1037/xlm0000050.

Hine, K., and Tsushima, Y. (2018). Not Explicit but Implicit Memory Is Influenced by Individual Perception Style. *PLOS One, 13*(1), 10. dx.doi.org.ezproxy.wpunj. edu/10.1371/journal.pone.0191654.

Hsin-I, L., Su-Ling,Y., Shinsuke, S., (2011). Novelty vs. Familiarity Principles in Preference Decisions: Task-Context of Past Experience Matters. *Frontiers in Psychology, 2*, 43– DOI=10.3389/fpsyg.2011.00043.

Jacoby, L. L. (1991). A Process Dissociation Framework: Separating Automatic from Intentional Uses of Memory. *Journal of Memory and Language, 30*(5), 513–541.

Jacoby, L. L., and Dallas, M. (1981). On the Relationship between Autobiographical Memory and Perceptual Learning. *Journal of Experimental Psychology: General, 110*(3), 306–340. dx.doi.org/10.1037/0096-3445.110.3.306.

Jacoby, L. L. and Kelley, C. 1994. Unconscious Influences of Memory: Dissociations and Automaticity. In *Consciousness and Cognition: Neuropsychological Perspectives*, Edited by Milner, D. and Rugg, M. London: Academic Press.

Jacoby, L. L., and Witherspoon, D. (1982). Remembering without Awareness. *Canadian Journal of Psychology/Revue Canadienne De Psychologie, 36*(2), 300–324. dx.doi. org/10.1037/h0080638.

Johnson, M. K. (1991). Reality Monitoring: Evidence from Confabulation in Organic Brain Disease Patients. *Awareness of Deficit After Brain Injury: Clinical and Theoretical Issues*, 176–97.

Johnson, M. K., Foley, M. A., and Leach, K. (1988). The Consequences for Memory of Imagining in Another Person's Voice. *Memory & Cognition, 16*(4), 337–342.

Johnson, M. K., Hashtroudi, S., and Lindsay, D. S. (1993). Source Monitoring. *Psychological Bulletin, 114*(1), 3.

Johnson, M. K., Kim, J. K., and Risse, G. (1985). Do Alcoholic Korsakoff's Syndrome Patients Acquire Affective reactions? *Journal of Experimental Psychology: Learning, Memory, and Cognition, 11*(1), 22.

Johnson, M. K., Raye, C. L., Wang, A. Y., and Taylor, T. H. (1979). Fact and Fantasy: The Roles of Accuracy and Variability in Confusing Imaginations with

Perceptual Experiences. *Journal of Experimental Psychology: Human Learning and Memory*, *5*(3), 229.

Jones, T., and Townsend, D. (2017). History and Future Technical Innovation in Positron Emission Tomography. *Journal of Medical Imaging* (Bellingham, WA), *4*(1), 011013–011013. doi.org/10.1117/1.jmi.4.1.011013.

Josephson, B. (1962). Possible New Effects in Superconductive Tunneling. *Physics Letters, 1*(7), 251–253. doi:10.1016/0031-9163(62)91369-0.

Kahneman, D. (2011). Thinking Fast and Slow. New York: Farrar, Straus and Giroux.

Kalra, P., Gabrieli, J., and Finn, A. (2019). Evidence of Stable Individual Differences in Implicit Learning. *Cognition, 190*, 199–211. doi.org/10.1016/j.cognition.2019.05.007.

Kapur, N., and Coughlan, A. K. (1980). Confabulation and Frontal Lobe Dysfunction. *Journal of Neurology, Neurosurgery and Psychiatry*, *43*(5), 461–463.

Kenzer, A. L., and Bishop, M. R. (2011). Evaluating Preference for Familiar and Novel Stimuli Across a Large Group of Children with Autism. *Research in Autism Spectrum Disorders, 5*(2), 819–825. doi: /dx.doi.org.ezproxy.wpunj.edu/10.1016/j.rasd.2010.09.011.

Kessler, R. C., Sonnega, A., Bromet, E., Hughes, M., and Nelson, C. B. (1995). Posttraumatic Stress Disorder in the National Comorbidity Survey. *Archives of General Psychiatry*, *52*(12), 1048–1060.

Kiefer, M. (2002). The N400 Is Modulated by Unconsciously Perceived Masked Words: Further Evidence for an Automatic Spreading Activation Account of N400 Priming Effects. *Brain Research. Cognitive Brain Research, 13*(1), 27–39doi.org/10.1016/S0926-6410(01)00085-4.

King, B., Dolfen, N., Gann, M., Renard, Z., Swinnen, S., and Albouy, G. (2019). Schema and Motor-Memory Consolidation. *Psychological Science*, *30*(7), 095679761984716–095679761984978. doi.org/10.1177/0956797619847164.

Kinoshita, S. (2003). The Nature of Masked Onset Priming Effects in Naming: A Review. In S. Kinoshita and S. J. Lupker (Eds.). *Masked Priming: The State of the Art*. New York: Psychology Press.

Kinoshita, S., and Lupker, S. J. (2003). *Masked priming: The State of the Art*. New York: Psychology Press.

Klauer, K. C., Schmitz, F., Teige-Mocigemba, S., and Voss, A. (2010). Understanding the Role of Executive Control in the Implicit Association Test: Why Flexible People Have Small IAT Effects. *Quarterly Journal of Experimental Psychology*, *63*(3), 595–619.

Knowlton, B. J., Mangels, J. A., and Squire, L. R. (1996). A Neostriatal Habit Learning System in Humans. *Science*, *273*(5280), 1399–1402. doi: 10.1126/science.273.5280.1399. PMID: 8703077.

Knowlton, B. J., Ramus, S. J., and Squire, L. R. (1992). Intact Artificial Grammar Learning in Amnesia: Dissociation of Classification Learning and Explicit Memory for Specific Instances. *Psychological Science, 3*(3), 172–179. doi.org/10.1111/j.1467-9280.1992.tb00021.x

Knowlton, B. J., and Squire, L. R. (1994). The Information Acquired During Artificial Grammar Learning. *Journal of Experimental Psychology: Learning, Memory, and Cognition, 20*(1), 79.

Knowlton, B. J., and Squire, L. R. (1996). Artificial Grammar Learning Depends on Implicit Acquisition of Both Abstract and Exemplar-Specific Information. *Journal of Experimental Psychology: Learning, Memory, and Cognition, 22*(1), 169.

Knutson, K. M., Wood, J. N., Spampinato, M. V., and Grafman, J. (2006). Politics on the Brain: An fMRI Investigation. *Social Neuroscience, 1*(1), 25–40.

Koen, J., and Yonelinas, A. (2014). The Effects of Healthy Aging, Amnestic Mild Cognitive Impairment, and Alzheimer's Disease on Recollection and Familiarity: A Meta-Analytic Review. *Neuropsychology Review, 24*(3), 332–354. doi.org/10.1007/s11065-014-9266-5.

Koenig, O., Thomas-Antérion, C., and Laurent, B. (1999). Procedural Learning in Parkinson's Disease: Intact and Impaired Cognitive Components. *Neuropsychologia, 37*(10), 1103–1109. doi.org/10.1016/S0028-3932(99)00040-8.

Kopelman, M. D. (1987). Two Types of Confabulation. *Journal of Neurology, Neurosurgery and Psychiatry, 50*(11), 1482–1487.

Kopelman, M. D. (1989). Remote and Autobiographical Memory, Temporal Context Memory and Frontal Atrophy in Korsakoff and Alzheimer patients. *Neuropsychologia, 27*(4), 437–460.

Koutstaal, W., Wagner, A., Rotte, M., Maril, A., Buckner, R., and Schacter, D. (2001). Perceptual Specificity in Visual Object Priming Functional Magnetic Resonance Imaging Evidence for a Laterality Difference in Fusiform Cortex. *Neuropsychologia, 39*(2), 184–199. doi.org/10.1016/S0028-3932(00)00087-7.

Kovarski, K., Mennella, R., Wong, S., Dunkley, B., Taylor, M., and Batty, M. (2019). Enhanced Early Visual Responses During Implicit Emotional Faces Processing in Autism Spectrum Disorder. *Journal of Autism and Developmental Disorders, 49*(3), 871–886. doi.org/10.1007/s10803-018-3787-3.

Kunst-Wilson, W. R., Zajonc, R. B. (1980). Affective Discrimination of Stimuli That Cannot Be Recognized. *Science, 207*(4430), 557–558. doi: 10.1126/science.7352271. PMID: 7352271.

Lacey, J. I. and Lacey, B. C. 1970. Some Autonomic-Central Nervous System Interrelationships. In *Physiological Correlates of Emotion*, edited by Black, P. 205–228. New York: Academic Press.

Lahne, J., Trubek, A., and Pelchat, M. (2014). Consumer Sensory Perception of Cheese Depends on Context: A Study Using Comment Analysis and Linear Mixed Models. *Food Quality and Preference, 32*, 184–197. doi.org/10.1016/j.foodqual.2013.10.007.

Landis, T., Regard, M., Bliestle, A., and Kleihues, P. (1988). Prosopagnosia and Agnosia for Noncanonical Views: An Autopsied Case. *Brain, 111*(6), 1287–1297.

Lang, P. J., Greenwald, M. K., Bradley, M. M., and Hamm, A. O. (1993). Looking at Pictures: Affective, Facial, Visceral, and Behavioral Reactions. *Psychophysiology, 30*(3), 261–273.

Lazarus, R. S., and McCleary, R., A. (1951). Autonomic Discrimination without Awareness: A Study of Subception. *Psychological Review, 58*(2), 113–122. doi: 10.1037/h0054104. PMID: 14834294.

Learmonth, A., Cuevas, K., and Rovee-Collier, C. (2015) Deconstructing the Reactivation of Imitation in Young Infants. *Psychology and Psychiatry Journal*, 301. doi.org/10.1002/dev.21298.

Lebrun, Y. (1987) Anosognosia in Aphasics. *Cortex, 23*, 251–263.

LeDoux, J. E. (1993). Emotional Memory: In Search of Systems and Synapses. In F. M. Crinella, and J. Yu (Eds.), *Brain Mechanisms: Papers in Memory of Robert Thompson*, 149–157. New York Academy of Sciences.

LeDoux, J. E. (1993). Emotional Memory Systems in the Brain. *Behavioral Brain Research, 58*(1–2), 69–79. doi: 10.1016/0166-4328(93)90091-4. PMID: 8136051.

LeDoux, J. E. (2012). Rethinking the Emotional Brain. *Neuron, 73*(4), 653–676. doi: 10.1016/j.neuron.2012.02.004. Erratum in: Neuron. 2012 Mar 8;73(5):1052. PMID: 22365542; PMCID: PMC3625946.

LeDoux, J. E. (2014). Coming to Terms with Fear. *Proceedings of the National Academy of Sciences of the United States of America, 111*(8), 2871–2878. doi: 10.1073/pnas.1400335111. Epub 2014 Feb 5. PMID: 24501122; PMCID: PMC3939902.

Lee, C. and Zhang, Y. (2018). Processing Lexical and Speaker Information in Repetition and Semantic/Associative Priming. *Journal of Psycholinguistic Research, 47*(1), 65–78. doi.org/10.1007/s10936-017-9514-y.

Legault, L., Green-Demers, I., Grant, P., and Chung, J. (2007). On the Self-Regulation of Implicit and Explicit Prejudice: A Self-Determination Theory Perspective. *Personality and Social Psychology Bulletin, 33*(5), 732–749.

Lhermitte, F., and Signoret, J. L. (1976). The Amnesic Syndromes and the Hippocampal-Mammillary System. In *Neural Mechanisms of Learning and Memory,* 49–56. Cambridge, MA: MIT Press.

Leopold, D. A. (2012). Primary Visual Cortex: Awareness and Blindsight. *Annual Review of Neuroscience, 35*, 91–109.

Levine, D., Buchsbaum, D., Hirsh-Pasek, K., Golinkoff, R. (2018). Finding Events in a Continuous World: A Developmental Account. *Developmental Psychobiology, 61*, 376–389. doi.org/10.1002/dev.21804.

Levy, B. A., and Kirsner, K. (1989). Reprocessing Text: Indirect Measures of Word and Message Level Processes. *Journal of Experimental Psychology: Learning, Memory, and Cognition, 15*(3), 407–417. dx.doi.org/10.1037/0278-7393.15.3.407.

Lundy, D., Allred, G., and Peebles, B. (2019). How Good Is This Song? Expert versus Nonexpert Aesthetic Appraisal. *Psychology of Aesthetics, Creativity, and the Arts, 13*(3), 293–304. doi.org/10.1037/aca0000181.

Lye, R. H., O'Boyle, D. J., Ramsden, R. T., Schady, W. (1988). Effects of a Unilateral Cerebellar Lesion on the Acquisition of Eye-Blink Conditioning in Man. *Journal of Physiology, 403*, 58P.

Madore, K., Thakral, P., Beaty, R., Addis, D., and Schacter, D. (2019). Neural Mechanisms of Episodic Retrieval Support Divergent Creative Thinking. *Cerebral Cortex, 29*(1), 150–166. doi.org/10.1093/cercor/bhx312.

Marcel, A. J. (1998). Blindsight and shape perception: Deficit of Visual Consciousness or of Visual Function? *Brain: A Journal of Neurology, 121*(8), 1565–1588.

Mayes, A. R. (1988). *Human Organic Memory Disorders, 7.* Cambridge University Press.

Mayes A. R., Pickering A., Fairbairn A. (1987). Amnesic Sensitivity to Proactive Interference: Its Relationship to Priming and the Causes of Amnesia. *Neuropsychologia, 25*(1B), 211–20. doi: 10.1016/0028-3932(87)90132-1. PMID: 3574659.

Meadows, J. C. (1974). The Anatomical Basis of Prosopagnosia. *Journal of Neurology, Neurosurgery and Psychiatry, 37*(5), 489–501.

McAndrews, M. P., Glisky, E. L., and Schacter, D. L. (1987). When Priming Persists: Long-Lasting Implicit Memory for a Single Episode in Amnesic Patients. *Neuropsychologia, 25*(3), 497–506.

McConnell, A. R., and Leibold, J. M. (2001). Relations Among the Implicit Association Test, Discriminatory Behavior, and Explicit Measures of Racial Attitudes. *Journal of Experimental Social Psychology, 37*(5), 435–442.

McDonald, R. J., Hong, N. S. (2004). A Dissociation of Dorso-Lateral Striatum and Amygdala Function on the Same Stimulus-Response Habit Task. *Neuroscience, 124*(3), 507–513. doi: 10.1016/j.neuroscience.2003.11.041. PMID: 14980722.

McGlynn, S.M. and Schacter, D.L (1989) Unawareness of Deficits in Neuropsychological Syndromes, *Journal of Clinical and Experimental Neuropsychology, 11*(2), 143–205, DOI: 10.1080/01688638908400882.

McNeil, J. E., and Warrington, E. K. (1991). Prosopagnosia: A Reclassification. *The Quarterly Journal of Experimental Psychology, 43*(2), 267–287.

Mierke, J., and Klauer, K. C. (2001). Implicit Association Measurement with the IAT: Evidence for Effects of Executive Control Processes. *Zeitschrift für Experimentelle Psychologie*.

Milner, B., Corkin, S., and Teuber, H. L. (1968). Further Analysis of the Hippocampal Amnesic Syndrome: 14-year Follow-Up Study of HM. *Neuropsychologia, 6*(3), 215–234.

Milner, B., Petrides, M., and Smith, M. L. (1985). Frontal Lobes and the Temporal Organization of Memory. *Human Neurobiology, 4*(3), 137–142.

Mishkin, M., Malamut, B., and Bachevalier, J. (1984). Memories and Habits: Two Neural Systems. *Neurobiology of Learning and Memory*, 65–77.

Mitchell, D., Kelly, C., and Brown, A. (2018). Replication and Extension of Long-Term Implicit Memory: Perceptual Priming but Conceptual Cessation. *Consciousness and Cognition, 58*, 1–9. doi.org/10.1016/j.concog.2017.12.002.

Moscovitch, M. (1985). Memory from Infancy to Old Age: Implications for Theories of Normal and Pathological Memory. *Annals of the New York Academy of Sciences, 444*(1), 78–96. doi.org/10.1111/j.1749-6632.1985.tb37581.x.

Moscovitch, M. (1989). Confabulation and the Frontal Systems: Strategic versus Associative Retrieval in Neuropsychological Theories of Memory. *Varieties of Memory and Consciousness: Essays in Honour of Endel Tulving*, 133–160. Hillsdale, NJ: Erlbaum

Moscovitch, M. (1995). Confabulation. In D. L. Schacter (Ed.), *Memory Distortions: How Minds, Brains, and Societies Reconstruct the Past*, 226–251. Cambridge, MA: Harvard University Press.

Moscovitch, M., and Melo, B. (1997). Strategic Retrieval and the Frontal Lobes: Evidence from Confabulation and Amnesia. *Neuropsychologia*, *35*(7), 1017–1034.

Mulligan, N. (2011). The Effect of Generation on Long-Term Repetition Priming in Auditory and Visual Perceptual Identification. *Acta Psychologica*, *137*(1), 18–23. doi.org/10.1016/j.actpsy.2011.02.001.

Myers, C. E., DeLuca, J., Schultheis, M. T., Schnirman, G. M., Ermita, B. R., Diamond, B. J., Warren, S. G. and Gluck, M. (2001). Impaired Delay Eyeblink Classical Conditioning in Individuals with Anterograde Amnesia Resulting from Anterior Communicating Artery Aneurysm. *Behavioral Neuroscience, 115*(3), 560–570.

Newcombe, F., Young, A. W., and De Haan, E. H. (1989). Prosopagnosia and Object Agnosia without Covert Recognition. *Neuropsychologia*, *27*(2), 179–191.

Newport, E. L. (2020). Children and Adults as Language Learners: Rules, Variation, and Maturational Change. *Topics in Cognitive Science*, *12*(1), 153–169.

Nishitani, N., Avikainen, S., and Hari, R. (2004). Abnormal Imitation-Related Cortical Activation Sequences in Asperger's Syndrome. *Annals of Neurology*, *55*(4), 558–562. doi.org/10.1002/ana.20031

Nissen, M. J., and Bullemer, P. (1987). Attentional Requirements of Learning: Evidence from Performance Measures. *Cognitive Psychology, 19*(1), 1–32. doi.org/10.1016/0010-0285(87)90002-8.

Nosek, B. A., Greenwald, A. G., and Banaji, M. R. (2007). The Implicit Association Test at Age 7: A Methodological and Conceptual Review. In J. A. Bargh (Ed.), *Social Psychology and the Unconscious: The Automaticity of Higher Mental Processes*, 265–292. New York: Psychology Press.

Ohman, A. (1979). The Orienting Response, Attention and Learning: An Information-Processing Response. *The Orienting Reflex in Humans*, 443–471.

Okada, Y., Lahteenmäki, A., and Xu, C. (1999). Experimental Analysis of Distortion of Magnetoencephalography Signals by the Skull. *Clinical Neurophysiology*, *110*(2), 230–238. doi.org/10.1016/S0013-4694(98)00099-6.

Olff, M., Langeland, W., Draijer, N., and Gersons, B. P. (2007). Gender Differences in Posttraumatic Stress Disorder. *Psychological Bulletin*, *133*(2), 183.

Onofrj M., Curatola L., Malatesta G., Bazzano S., Colamartino P, Fulgente T. (1991). Reduction of P3 Latency during Outcome from Posttraumatic Amnesia. *Acta Neurologica Scandinavica*, *83*(5), 273–279. doi: 10.1111/j.1600-0404.1991.tb04700.x. PMID: 2063648.

Overgaard, M. (2012). Blindsight: Recent and Historical Controversies on the Blindness of Blindsight. *Wiley Interdisciplinary Reviews: Cognitive Science*, *3*(6), 607–614.

Overgaard, M. (2011). Visual Experience and Blindsight: A Methodological Review. *Experimental Brain Research*, *209*(4), 473–479.

Packard, M. G., and Goodman, J. (2012). Emotional Arousal and Multiple Memory Systems in the Mammalian Brain. *Frontiers in Behavioral Neuroscience, 6*, 9. dx.doi.org/10.3389/fnbeh.2012.00014.

Packard, M. G., & McGaugh, J. L. (1992). Double Dissociation of Fornix and Caudate Nucleus Lesions on Acquisition of Two Water Maze Tasks: Further Evidence for Multiple Memory Systems. *Behavioral Neuroscience*, *106*(3), 439–446.

Paller, K. A., Mayes, A. R., Thompson, K. M., Young, A. W., Roberts, J., and Meudell, P. R. (1992). Priming of Face Matching in Amnesia. *Brain and Cognition*, *18*(1), 46–59. dx.doi.org/10.1016/0278-2626(92)90110-8.

Paller, K. A., and Kutas, M. (1992). Brain Potentials during Memory Retrieval Provide Neurophysiological Support for the Distinction between Conscious Recollection and Priming. *Journal of Cognitive Neuroscience*, *4*(4), 375–392.

Paller, K. A., Kutas, M., and Mayes, A. R. (1987). Neural Correlates of Encoding in an Incidental Learning Paradigm. *Electroencephalography and Clinical Neurophysiology*, *67*(4), 360–371.

Panouillères, M., Tofaris, G., Brown, P., and Jenkinson, N. (2016). Intact Acquisition and Short-Term Retention of Non-Motor Procedural Learning in Parkinson's Disease. *PLOS One*, *11*(2), e0149224–e0149224. doi.org/10.1371/journal.pone.0149224.

Park, J., and Donaldson, D. (2016). Investigating the Relationship between Implicit and Explicit Memory: Evidence that Masked Repetition Priming Speeds the Onset of Recollection. *NeuroImage* (Orlando, FL), *139*, 8–16. doi.org/10.1016/j.neuroimage.2016.06.013.

Parker, A., Powell, D., and Dagnall, N. (2018). Effects of Saccade Induced Retrieval Enhancement on Conceptual and Perceptual Tests of Explicit and Implicit Memory. *Brain and Cognition*, *121*, 1–10. doi.org/10.1016/j.bandc.2017.12.002.

Parkin, A. J. (1996). Focal Retrograde Amnesia: A Multi-Faceted Disorder? *Acta Neurologica Belgica*, *96*(1), 43–50. Retrieved from psycnet.apa.org/record/1997-02981-002.

Payne, B. K. (2005). Conceptualizing Control in Social Cognition: How Executive Functioning Modulates the Expression of Automatic Stereotyping. *Journal of Personality and Social Psychology*, *89*(4), 488.

Payne, P., Levine, P. A., and Crane-Godreau, M. A. (2015). Somatic Experiencing: Using Interoception and Proprioception as Core Elements of Trauma Therapy. *Frontiers in Psychology*, *6*, 93.

Perruchet, P., and Pacton, S. (2006). Implicit Learning and Statistical Learning: One Phenomenon, Two Approaches. *Trends in Cognitive Sciences*, *10*(5), 233–238.

Phelps, E. A., O'Connor, K. J., Cunningham, W. A., Funayama, E. S., Gatenby, J. C., Gore, J. C., and Banaji, M. R. (2000). Performance on Indirect Measures of Race Evaluation Predicts Amygdala Activation. *Journal of Cognitive Neuroscience*, *12*(5), 729–738.

Phelps, E. A., Cannistraci, C. J., and Cunningham, W. A. (2003). Intact Performance on an Indirect Measure of Race Bias Following Amygdala Damage. *Neuropsychologia*, *41*(2), 203–208.

Phillips, W. J., Hine, D. W., and Thorsteinsson, E. B. (2010). Implicit Cognition and Depression: A Meta-Analysis. *Clinical Psychology Review*, *30*(6), 691–709. doi.org/10.1016/j.cpr.2010.05.002.

Plouffe, L., and Stelmack, R. M. (1984). The Electrodermal Orienting Response and Memory: An Analysis of Age Differences in Picture Recall. *Psychophysiology, 2 1*(2), 191–198.

Raichle, M. and Posner, M. (1997). Behind the Scenes of Functional Brain Imaging: A Historical and Physiological Perspective. *Proceedings of the National Academy of Sciences - PNAS, 95*(3), 765–772. doi.org/10.1073/pnas.95.3.765.

Rapcsak, S. Z., Kaszniak, A. W., Reminger, S. L., Glisky, M. L., Glisky, E. L., and Comer, J. F. (1998). Dissociation between Verbal and Autonomic Measures of Memory Following Frontal Lobe Damage. *Neurology, 50*(5), 1259–1265.

Rauch, S., Savage, C., Alpert, N., Dougherty, D., Kendrick, A., Curran, T., Brown, H., Manzo, P., Fischman, A., and Jenike, M. (1997). Probing Striatal Function in Obsessive-Compulsive Disorder: A PET Study of Implicit Sequence Learning. *The Journal of Neuropsychiatry and Clinical Neurosciences, 9*(4), 568–573. doi. org/10.1176/jnp.9.4.568.

Reber, A. S. (1967). Implicit Learning of Artificial Grammars. *Journal of Verbal Learning and Verbal Behavior, 6*(6), 855–863. doi.org/10.1016/ s0022-5371(67)80149-x.

Reeder, P. A., Newport, E. L., and Aslin, R. N. (2013). From Shared Contexts to Syntactic Categories: The Role of Distributional Information in Learning Linguistic Form-Classes. *Cognitive Psychology, 66*(1), 30–54.

Rees-Nishio, M. (1985). *Memory, Emotion, and Skin Conductance Responses in Young and Elderly Normal and Memory-Impaired People,* available from APA PsycInfo®. (617209797; 1986–52717–001).

Reinitz, M. T., and Alexander, R. (1996). Mechanisms of Facilitation in Primed Perceptual Identification. *Memory & Cognition, 24*(2), 129–135.

Rémillard, S., Pourcher, E., and Cohen, H. (2010). Long-Term Skill Proceduralization in Schizophrenia. *Journal of the International Neuropsychological Society, 16*(1), 148–156. doi.org/10.1017/S1355617709991123.

Renault, B., Signoret, J. L., Debruille, B., Breton, F., and Bolgert, F. (1989). Brain Potentials Reveal Covert Facial Recognition in Prosopagnosia. *Neuropsychologia , 27*(7), 905–912.

Reite, M. and Zimmerman, J. (1978). Magnetic Phenomena of the Central Nervous System. *Annual Review of Biophysics and Bioengineering, 7,* 167–188. doi. org/10.1146/annurev.bb.07.060178.001123.

Richeson, J. A., Baird, A. A., Gordon, H. L., Heatherton, T. F., Wyland, C. L., Trawalter, S., and Shelton, J. N. (2003). An fMRI Investigation of the Impact of Interracial Contact on Executive Function. *Nature Neuroscience, 6*(12), 1323–1328.doi.org/10.1038/nn1156.

Richeson, J. A., and Nussbaum, R. J. (2004). The Impact of Multiculturalism versus Color-Blindness on Racial Bias. *Journal of Experimental Social Psychology, 40*(3), 417–423.

Ro, T., and Rafal, R. (2006). Visual Restoration in Cortical Blindness: Insights from Natural and TMS-Induced Blindsight. *Neuropsychological Rehabilitation, 16*(4), 377–396.

Robertson, E. (2007). The Serial Reaction Time Task: Implicit Motor Skill Learning? *The Journal of Neuroscience*, *27*(38), 10073–10075. doi.org/10.1523/jneurosci.2747-07.2007.

Romberg, A. R., and Saffran, J. R. (2010). Statistical Learning and Language Acquisition. doi.org/10.1002/wcs.78.

Rooke, S. E., Hine, D. W., and Thorsteinsson, E. B. (2008). Implicit Cognition and Substance Use: A Meta-Analysis. *Addictive Behaviors*, *33*(10), 1314–1328. doi.org/10.1016/j.addbeh.2008.06.009.

Roth, W. T. (1983). 8 A Comparison of P300 and Skin Conductance Response. In *Advances in Psychology, 10*, 177–199). North-Holland.

Rovee-Collier, C. (1997). Dissociations in infant memory: Rethinking the development of implicit and explicit memory. *Psychological Review*, 104(3), 467–498. doi.org/10.1037/0033-295X.104.3.467.

Rovee-Collier, C., and Cuevas, K. (2009). Multiple Memory Systems Are Unnecessary to Account for Infant Memory Development: An Ecological Model. *Developmental Psychology*, *45*(1), 160–174. doi.org/10.1037/a0014538.

Rovee-Collier, C., Hayne, H., and Colombo, M. (2001). The Development of Implicit and Explicit Memory. Amsterdam/Philadelphia: John Benjamins.

Rousey, C., and Holzman, P. S. (1967). Recognition of One's Own Voice. *Journal of Personality and Social Psychology, 6*(4), 464–466. dx.doi.org/10.1037/h0024837.

Saffran, J. (2018). Statistical Learning as a Window into Developmental Disabilities. *Journal of Neurodevelopmental Disorders, 10*(1), 35–35.

Saffran, J. R., Aslin, R. N., and Newport, E. L. (1996). Statistical Learning by 8-Month-Old Infants. *Science*, *274*(5294), 1926–1928.

Salmon, D. P., and Heindel, W. C. (2014). Word-Stem Completion Priming in Alzheimer's Disease. In L. Nilsson, and N. Ohta (Eds.), *Dementia and Memory; Dementia and Memory,* 225–245. New York: Psychology Press. Retrieved from ezproxy.wpunj.edu/login?url=search.proquest.com/docview/1634753739?a.

Schacter, D. L. (1987). Memory, Amnesia, and Frontal Lobe Dysfunction. *Psychobiology*, *15*(1), 21–36.

Schacter, D. L. (1987). Implicit Memory: History and Current Status. *Journal of Experimental Psychology: Learning, Memory, and Cognition, 13*(3), 501–518. dx.doi.org/10.1037/0278-7393.13.3.501.

Schacter, D. L. (2019). Implicit Memory, Constructive Memory, and Imagining the Future: A Career Perspective. *Perspectives on Psychological Science, 14*(2), 256–272. dx.doi.org/10.1177/1745691618803640.

Schacter, D., Dobbins, I., and Schnyer, D. (2004). Specificity of Priming: A Cognitive Neuroscience Perspective. *Nature Reviews. Neuroscience*, *5*(11), 853–862. doi.org/10.1038/nrn1534.

Schacter, D., and Graf, P. (1989). Modality Specificity of Implicit Memory for New Associations. *Journal of Experimental Psychology. Learning, Memory, and Cognition*, *15*(1), 3–12. doi.org/10.1037/0278-7393.15.1.3.

Schendan, H. E. (2019). Memory Influences Visual Cognition across Multiple Functional States of Interactive Cortical Dynamics. In Kara D. Federmeier (Ed).

Psychology of Learning and Motivation, *71*, 303–386. Cambridge, MA: Academic Press. doi.org/10.1016/bs.plm.2019.07.00.

Schnider, A., and Ptak, R. (1999). Spontaneous Confabulators Fail to Suppress Currently Irrelevant Memory Traces. *Nature Neuroscience*, *2*(7), 677–681.

Sebastiani, L., Castellani, E., Gemignani, A., Artoni, F., and Menicucci, D. (2015). Inefficient Stimulus Processing at Encoding Affects Formation of High-Order General Representation: A Study on Cross-Modal Word-Stem Completion Task. *Brain Research*, *1622*, 386–396. doi.org/10.1016/j.brainres.2015.06.042.

Segal, Z. V. (1996). Cognitive Interference in Depressive and Anxiety Based Disorders. In I. Sarason, G. Pierce, and R. Gregory (Eds.), *Cognitive Interference: Theories, Methods, and Findings*, 325–345. Mahwah, NJ: Lawrence Erlbaum.

Sergent, J., and Poncet, M. (1990). From Covert to Overt Recognition of Faces in a Prosopagnosic Patient. *Brain*, *113*(4), 989–1004.

Sergent, J., and Villemure, J. G. (1989). Prosopagnosia in a Right Hemispherectomized Patient. *Brain*, *112*(4), 975–995.

Shapiro, B. E., Alexander, M. P., Gardner, H., and Mercer, B. (1981). Mechanisms of Confabulation. *Neurology*, *31*(9), 1070–1070.

Shimamura, A. P. (1986). Priming Effects in Amnesia: Evidence for a Dissociable Memory Function. *The Quarterly Journal of Experimental Psychology Section A*, *38*(4), 619–644.

Shimamura, A. P., Janowsky, J. S., and Squire, L. R. (1991). What Is the Role of Frontal Lobe Damage in Memory Disorders? In H. S. Levin, H. M. Eisenberg, and A. L. Benton (Eds.), *Frontal Lobe Function and Dysfunction*, 173–195. New York: Oxford University Press.

Shimamura A. P., Squire L. R. (1984). Paired-Associate Learning and Priming Effects in Amnesia: A Neuropsychological Study. *Journal of Experimental Psychology: General*, *113*(4), 556–570. doi: 10.1037//0096-3445.113.4.556. PMID: 6240522.

Shimamura, A. P., and Squire, L. R. (1987). A Neuropsychological Study of Fact Memory and Source Amnesia. *Journal of Experimental Psychology: Learning, Memory, and Cognition*, *13*(3), 464.

Siddle, D. A. (1991). Orienting, Habituation, and Resource Allocation: An Associative Analysis. *Psychophysiology*, *28*(3), 245–259.

Silva, S., Folia, V., Inácio, F., Castro, S., and Petersson, K. (2018). Modality Effects in Implicit Artificial Grammar Learning: An EEG Study. *Brain Research*, *1687*, 50–59. doi.org/10.1016/j.brainres.2018.02.020.

Silver, A. H., and Zimmerman, J. E. (1965). Quantum Transitions and Loss in Multiply Connected Superconductors. *Physical Review Letters*, *15*, 888–891. doi. org/10.1103/PhysRevLett.15.888   .

Smith, J., Johnston, J., Musgrave, R., Zakrzewski, A., Boomer, J., Church, B., and Ashby, F. (2014). Cross-Modal Information Integration in Category Learning. *Attention, Perception & Psychophysics*, *76*(5), 1473–1484. doi. org/10.3758/s13414-014-0659-6.

Sokolov, E. N. 1963. *Perception and the Conditional Reflex*, New York: MacMillan.

Sopp, M. R., Brueckner, A. H, Schäfer, S. K., Lass-Hennemann, J. and Michael, T. (2019). Differential Effects of Sleep on Explicit and Implicit Memory for Potential

Trauma Reminders: Findings from an Analogue Study, *European Journal of Psychotraumatology, 10*(1), 1644128, DOI: 10.1080/20008198.2019.1644128.

Spence, C., and Deroy, O. (2013). How Automatic are Crossmodal Correspondences? *Consciousness and Cognition, 22*(1), 245–260. doi.org/10.1016/j.concog.2012.12.006.

Squire, L. R. (1987). *Memory and Brain.* New York: Oxford University Press.

Squire, L. (2004). Memory Systems of the Brain: A Brief History and Current Perspective. *Neurobiology of Learning and Memory, 82*(3), 171–177. doi.org/10.1016/j.nlm.2004.06.005.

Squire, L. R., Cohen, N. J., and Zouzounis, J. A. (1984). Preserved Memory in Retrograde Amnesia: Sparing of a Recently Acquired Skill. *Neuropsychologia, 22*(2), 145–152. dx.doi.org/10.1016/0028-3932(84)90057-5.

Squire, L. R., and McKee, R. (1992). Influence of Prior Events on Cognitive Judgments in Amnesia. *Journal of Experimental Psychology: Learning, Memory, and Cognition, 18*(1), 106.

Stacy, A. W., and Wiers, R. W. (2010). Implicit Cognition and Addiction: A Tool for Explaining Paradoxical Behavior. *Annual Review of Clinical Psychology, 6*, 551–575. doi.org/10.1146/annurev.clinpsy.121208.131444.

Stormark, K. M. (2004). Skin Conductance and Heart-Rate Responses as Indices of Covert Face Recognition in Preschool Children. *Infant and Child Development: An International Journal of Research and Practice, 13*(5), 423–433.

Strauss, H., Zaret, B., Pieri, P., and Lahiri, A. (2017). George De Hevesy, Recipient of the 1943 Nobel Prize for Chemistry. *Journal of Nuclear Cardiology, 24*(6), 1848–1849. doi.org/10.1007/s12350-017-1041-6.

Stuss, D. T., Benson, D. F., Clermont, R., Della Malva, C. L., Kaplan, E. F., and Weir, W. S. (1986). Language Functioning After Bilateral Prefrontal Leukotomy. *Brain and Language, 28*(1), 66–70.

Taesler, P., Jablonowski, J., Fu, Q., and Rose, M. (2019). Modeling Implicit Learning in a Cross-Modal Audio-Visual Serial Reaction Time Task. *Cognitive Systems Research, 54*, 154–164. doi.org/10.1016/j.cogsys.2018.10.002.

Talland, G. A. (1965). *Deranged Memory: A Psychonomic Study of the Amnesic Syndrome.* United Kingdom: Academic Press.

Talland, G. A., Sweet, W. H., and Ballentine Jr, H. T. (1967). Amnesic Syndrome with Anterior Communicating Artery Aneurism. *The Journal of Nervous and Mental Disease, 145*(3), 179–192.

Teachman, B. A., Cody, M. W., and Clerkin, E. M. (2010). Clinical Applications of Implicit Social Cognition Theories and Methods. In B. Gawronski and B. K. Payne (Eds.), Handbook of Implicit Social Cognition: Measurement, Theory, and Applications, 489–521. New York: The Guilford Press.

Teachman B. A., and Woody S. R. (2004). Staying Tuned to Research in Implicit Cognition: Relevance for Clinical Practice with Anxiety Disorders. *Cognitive and Behavioral Practice 1 1, 149–159, 2004.* dx.doi.org/10.1016/S1077-7229(04)80026-9.

Thakral, P. P., Kensinger, E. A., Slotnick, S. D. (2016). Familiarity and Priming are Mediated by Overlapping Neural Substrates. *Brain Research, 1632*, 107–118. doi: 10.1016/j.brainres.2015.12.008. Epub 2015 Dec 10. PMID: 26683080.

Thiessen, E. D., and Erickson, L. C. (2013). Beyond Word Segmentation: A Two-Process Account of Statistical Learning. *Current Directions in Psychological Science, 22*(3), 239–243.

Thiessen, E. D., and Saffran, J. R. (2003). When Cues Collide: Use of Stress and Statistical Cues to Word Boundaries by 7-to 9-Month-Old Infants. *Developmental Psychology, 39*(4), 706.

Tolin, D. F., and Foa, E. B. (2006). Sex Differences in Trauma and Posttraumatic Stress Disorder: A Quantitative Review of 25 Years of Research. *Psychological Bulletin, 132*(6), 959–992. dx.doi.org/10.1037/0033-2909.132.6.959.

Tonelli, A., Gori, M., and Brayda, L. (2016). The Influence of Tactile Cognitive Maps on Auditory Space Perception in Sighted Persons. *Frontiers in Psychology, 7*, 1683. doi.org/10.3389/fpsyg.2016.01683.

Tranel, D., and Damasio, A. R. (1985). Knowledge without Awareness: An Autonomic Index of Facial Recognition by Prosopagnosics. *Science, 228*(4706), 1453–1454. dx.doi.org/10.1126/science.4012303

Tranel, D., and Damasio, A. R. (1988). Non-Conscious Face Recognition in Patients with Face Agnosia. *Behavioural Brain Research, 30*(3), 235–249.

Tranel, D., Fowles, D. C., and Damasio, A. R. (1985). Electrodermal Discrimination of Familiar and Unfamiliar Faces: A Methodology. *Psychophysiology, 22*(4), 403–408.

Tulving, E., and Schacter, D. (1990). Priming and Human Memory Systems. *Science (American Association for the Advancement of Science), 247*(4940), 301–306. doi. org/10.1126/science.2296719.

Vakil, E., and Lev-Ran Galon, C. (2014). Baseline Performance and Learning Rate of Conceptual and Perceptual Skill-Learning Tasks: The Effect of Moderate to Severe Traumatic Brain Injury. *Journal of Clinical and Experimental Neuropsychology, 36*(5), 447–454. doi.org/10.1080/13803395.2014.901299.

Vallet, G. T., Hudon, C., Simard, M., and Versace, R. (2013). The Disconnection Syndrome in the Alzheimer's Disease: The Cross-Modal Priming Example. *Cortex, 49*(9), 2402–2415. doi.org/10.1016/j.cortex.2012.10.010.

van den Heuvel, M. P., Pol, H. E. H. (2010). Exploring the Brain Network: A Review on Resting-State fMRI Functional Connectivity, *European Neuropsychopharmacology, 20* (8), 519–534, doi.org/10.1016/j.euroneuro.2010.03.008.

Van der kolk, B. A. (2006). Clinical Implications of Neuroscience Research in PTSD, *Annals of the New York Academy of Sciences*, 1–17.

van der Kleij, S., Groen, M., Segers, E., and Verhoeven, L. (2019). Enhanced Semantic Involvement during Word Recognition in Children with Dyslexia. *Journal of Experimental Child Psychology, 178*, 15–29. doi.org/10.1016/j.jecp.2018.09.006.

Verbaten, M. N. (1983). 9 The Influence of Information on Habituation of Cortical, Autonomic and Behavioral Components of the Orienting Response (OR). In *Advances in Psychology, 10*, 201–216. North-Holland.

Verfaellie, M., Bauer, R. M., and Bowers, D. (1991). Autonomic and Behavioral Evidence of "Implicit" Memory in Amnesia. *Brain and Cognition, 15*(1), 10–25. dx.doi.org/10.1016/0278-2626(91)90012-W.

Vöhringer, I., Kolling, T., Graf, F., Poloczek, S., Fassbender, I., Freitag, C., Lamm, B., Suhrke, J., Teiser, J., Teubert, M., Keller, H., Lohaus, A., Schwarzer, G., and Knopf, M. (2018). The Development of Implicit Memory from Infancy to Childhood: On Average Performance Levels and Interindividual Differences. *Child Development, 89*(2), 370–382. doi.org/10.1111/cdev.12749.

Vriezen, E. R., and Moscovitch, M. (1990). Memory for Temporal Order and Conditional Associative-Learning in Patients with Parkinson's Disease. *Neuropsychologia, 28*(12), 1283–1293.

Wagner, A. D., and Gabrieli, J. D. (1998). On the Relationship between Recognition Familiarity and Perceptual Fluency: Evidence for Distinct Mnemonic Processes. *Acta Psychologica, 98*(2–3), 211–230.

Wagner, A. R. (1978). Expectancies and the Priming of STM. In Hulse, S. H., Fowler, H., and Honig, W. K. (Eds.). (1978). *Cognitive Processes in Animal Behavior* (1st ed.). Routledge. doi.org/10.4324/9780203710029.

Walk, A., and Conway, C. (2016). Cross-Domain Statistical–Sequential Dependencies Are Difficult to Learn. *Frontiers in Psychology, 7*, 250–250. doi.org/10.3389/fpsyg.2016.00250.

Wang, Y., Wang, Y., Liu, P., Wang, J., Gong, Y., Di, M., and Li, Y. (2018). Critical Role of Top-Down Processes and the Push-Pull Mechanism in Semantic Single Negative priming. *Consciousness and Cognition, 57*, 84–93. doi.org/10.1016/j.concog.2017.11.007.

Warrington, E., and Weiskrantz, L. (1970). Amnesic Syndrome: Consolidation or Retrieval? *Nature, 228*, 628–630. doi.org/10.1038/228628a0.

Warrington, E.K. and Weiskrantz, L. (1982). Amnesia: A Disconnection Syndrome? *Neuropsychologia, 20*, 233–248. doi.org/10.1016/0028-3932(82)90099-9.

Was, C., Woltz, D., Hirsch, D., and Hirsch, D. (2019). Memory Processes Underlying Long-Term Semantic Priming. *Memory & Cognition, 47*(2), 313–325. doi.org/10.3758/s13421-018-0867-8.

Weiskrantz, L., and Warrington, E. K. (1979). Conditioning in Amnesic Patients. *Neuropsychologia, 17*(2), 187–194. dx.doi.org/10.1016/0028-3932(79)90009-5.

Wiers, R. W., Stacy, A. W., Ames, S. L., Noll, J. A., Sayette, M. A., Zack, M., and Krank, M. (2002). Implicit and Explicit Alcohol-Related Cognitions. *Alcoholism, Clinical and Experimental Research, 26*(1), 129–137.

Willingham, D., Salidis, J., and Gabrieli, J. (2002). Direct Comparison of Neural Systems Mediating Conscious and Unconscious Skill Learning. *Journal of Neurophysiology, 88*(3), 1451–1460. doi.org/10.1152/jn.2002.88.3.1451.

Wilson, T. D., Lindsey, S., and Schooler, T. Y. (2000). A Model of Dual Attitudes. *Psychological Review, 107*(1), 101.

Yonelinas, A. P. (2001). Components of Episodic Memory: The Contribution of Recollection and Familiarity. *Philosophical Transactions of the Royal Society of London. Series B: Biological Sciences, 356*(1413), 1363–1374.

Young, A. W., and De Haan, E. H. (1988). Boundaries of Covert Recognition in Prosopagnosia. *Cognitive Neuropsychology*, *5*(3), 317–336.

Young, A. W., & De Haan, E. H. (1992). Face Recognition and Awareness after Brain Injury. in *The Neuropsychology of Consciousness*, Academic Press, 69–90.

Young, A. W., and Ellis, H. D. (1989). Childhood Prosopagnosia. *Brain and Cognition*, *9*(1), 16–47.

Index

About the Authors

Bruce J. Diamond is professor of psychology at William Paterson University and a clinical-research neuropsychologist. He is the author of research articles on neurologic, neurodevelopmental and neuropsychiatric disorders including work on memory, aware and unaware, executive function, and information processing using computer-based, psychophysiological and pharmacological techniques. He sits on the Editorial Board of Archives in Clinical Neuropsychology.

Amy E. Learmonth is professor of psychology at William Paterson University and a developmental psychologist. She is the author of articles on spatial ability, imitation, and memory in infants and young children and a past president of the Eastern Psychological Association. Her research interests have recently expanded to include young children with autism and neurodiversity aspects of development.

Katherine Makarec is professor of psychology at William Paterson University and a cognitive psychologist. Her research interests can be conceptualized into two domains, emotion and memory and the interaction of emotional tone with information encoding. And the second is the history of psychology especially around its founding and early modern times, from Fechner to the Von Restorff effect and its application to how emotional occurrences disproportionally impact memory encoding. That is how isolated emotional occurrences disproportionally impact on encoding into memory.

www.ingramcontent.com/pod-product-compliance
Lightning Source LLC
Chambersburg PA
CBHW022325280326
41932CB00010B/1236